WILD BENNET BURLEIGH
THE PEN AND THE PISTOL

For Ciara and Cuan.

Copyright © September 2012 by Graeden Greaves
All rights reserved.
ISBN-10: 1478155973
ISBN-13: 978-1478155973
Library of Congress Control Number: 2012915735

CONTENTS

Chapter 1	The Early Years	4
Chapter 2	The American Civil War	
	Part A - Go West Young Man	8
	Part B - Guerrillas on Lake Erie.	15
	Part C - Arrest and Extradition	25
	Part D - The American trial	40
Chapter 3	The Sudan	
	Part A- First steps in Africa	52
	Part B - The road to Omdurman	74
	Part C – Reconquering the Sudan	83
Chapter 4	Madagascar 1894	97
Chapter 5	The Ashantee Kingdom 1895-6	105
Chapter 6	The Great Boer War 1899-1902	112
Chapter 7	Russia / Japan War 1904-5	136
Chapter 8	Other campaigns and incidents	145
Chapter 9	Between The Wars	
	Part A – The Home Front	152
	Part B – Burleigh the liberal imperialist	161
	Part C – Family Life	168
Chapter 10	Burleigh puts down his pen	176
	Sources	181

Bennet Burleigh, who had fought for the independence of the South during the Civil War in America, bluff and kindly, with a heart too big for his body, bursting with kindness and good nature, endowed with remarkable energy and pluck, and with as much knowledge of soldiering as most generals, was a striking figure." – Melton Prior. (War Artist and friend.)

Chapter 1 - The early years.

As a child, my grandmother Euphemia, the great-granddaughter of Bennet Burleigh used to tell us somewhat diluted stories of the exploits of a man whom her own grandmother, Burleighs daughter, referred to as a "bad, bad man". As a child these tales of adventures in foreign lands both frightened and inspired.

Burleighs life was to span Britain's golden age which saw the country dominate overseas markets with a strategy of informal colonialism; causing the spread of the English language, the British Imperial system of measures, and rules for commodity markets based on English common law. Burleigh was also to be a product of his time, in 1844, the first press telegram in Britain was sent to The Times announcing the birth of Prince Alfred to Queen Victoria and the ever expanding growth of the railways led to the growth of national daily newspapers. Burleigh was perhaps one of the most famous Victorian's who is largely unheard of today. He was a consort to Kings and Queens, and friends with other people whose fame has lasted a little longer, such as Kipling, Churchill and Conan Doyle. In the 64 years that followed Queen Victoria's Coronation in 1838, not one passed without military action in the interests of the Empire; which at the time, was the largest the world had ever known, and Burleigh was a war correspondent with the Daily Telegraph during this time; Today we have multiple 24 hour streaming live news, but things then were a little different, no TV, no radio, the only news the masses got, was perhaps the copy of a newspaper after Sunday service. The main man in journalism was Burleigh, he was widely labelled as the greatest of all correspondents; a veteran of such campaigns as the American Civil War, The Sudanese wars and the Boer War. Fighting was done the old fashioned way, hand to hand, and on horseback and the stories were sent by telegraph to get the news to the people first. Burleigh died on the eve of World War One, and the ensuing carnage ensured that his legend was set to slumber.

Bennet Graham Burley (He changed his name to Burleigh after the American Civil War) was born in 1840 in Glasgow, Scotland, to Robert Burley and Christian Seath, and according to the 1861 census, he was to be one of 6 children over the next 14 years, Agnes, Elizabeth, Christina, Robert and James - though it seems Elizabeth died in childhood. His parents were local people spending most of their lives around the Gorbals, though his father originally hailed from Bo 'ness.

By the middle of the 20th century, Robert Burley and Sons, were one of the oldest handle makers in Scotland who were also noted for every method of the bending and turning of wood, specialising in a range of products from mallet heads, pickaxe handles, spades and shovels, to making a few boneshaker wooden bicycles on the side. Robert had been born in 1806 and received his early education in Greenock, near Glasgow. The River Clyde which runs through Glasgow supported at the time, a huge shipbuilding and sailing industry. Roberts own father had been a sailor, but it seems the younger man decided he would rather make than sail ships. When Robert finished his schooling he became an apprentice to the block making branch of the Messers. Steeles shipbuilding yard, rising eventually to the position of foreman. In 1839, whilst still in his early thirties, Burley decided to go into business for himself, and set up a small shop in Tradeston with a partner, who pulled out after three years, leaving Burley with a couple of journeymen joiners to make the wooden blocks that were in great demand in the shipping industry at the time, all the products were made by the means of foot powered lathes and circular saws.

ROBERT BURLEYS FACTORY IN BUSIER DAYS.

Business improved steadily and a few adjacent units were taken over, Fifteen or so years later, the Glasgow Directory listed "Robert Burley and Company, joiners, blockmakers, turners, and hammer handle manufacturers by steam power".

The growth in business meant larger premises were required. A green field sight was procured, and a new brick mill of two storeys was built. The upper floor held some twenty lathes for turning, and down below the wood was cut. This building was burnt down in July 1891, with the damages valued at £3,000. Another site was found, and in 1892 another larger property was built, and Robert's son James eventually took over. During World War 1 the firm was inundated with extra orders from the War Office, Admiralty and Colonial Office, which came on top of their usually business of supplying the railways, collieries and shipyards. The business managed to reach its centenary, but is no more. The building still stands, though somewhat dilapidated now, and is located in the shadow of Glasgow Rangers Ibrox Stadium.

Robert Burley was also a trustee of Glasgow's Mechanics Institution, and, after decades of hard work, was largely responsible for the opening of the Greenock Mechanics Library in 1840. At the opening, Mr Burley, who regularly attended the lectures of the Institution of Arts and Science some years prior to the founding of the Library, spoke of his pleasant connection with the Institution, and rejoiced that the labour and love of long gone-bye days had not been without fruit.

According to Ben Burleys own account, after he left school in Glasgow he joined his fathers company as an apprentice joiner rising to the position of journeyman, and then spent some time, like many other young men born by the Clyde in the shipping industry, where he worked as a shipping clerk. In the early 1860's a Victorian soldier of fortune, and childhood friend of Burleigh, named MacIver and several of his friends left Scotland and headed for the seat of the Italian war. MacIver entered Naples with the "Liberator" Garibaldi in September 1860. Garibaldi then entrusted MacIver with a mission to Scotland for the purpose of organising a Scottish company. McIver's flying visit home was so successful that he was able to return to the seat of war with a contingent of men, and being swayed by his bravado, and the lure of war, which was for many young men of his age, the only way to satisfy their need for adventure, Burleigh joined up and went to Italy to fight for Garibaldi, but then turned sides and fought against him for the Papal Guards. This story was later corroborated by an American Newspaper during his later Civil War trial.

After a few more years working with his father, the American Civil War started, and Burleigh, with a young mans nose for adventure headed to America, where he volunteered to follow the fortunes of the defeated cause.

Chapter 2 - The America Civil War
Part A - Go West Young Man

The American Civil War (1861–1865) was a conflict between the United States, the Northern Union, and the Southern states of the newly-formed Confederate States of America. Under the leadership of Abraham Lincoln, the Republicans were opposed to the expansion of slavery in territories owned by the United States, and their victory in the presidential election of 1860 led seven Southern states to declare their secession from the Union, who in turn regarded the act as a rebellion. Hostilities began in April 1861, when Confederate forces attacked a U.S. military installation at Fort Sumter in South Carolina; four more Southern states then declared their secession. After many battles, General Lee's reverse at Gettysburg in early July 1863 proved a turning point. The Confederate resistance had collapsed by the time Lee surrendered to Grant at the Appomattox Court House in April 1865. The war caused the death of 620,000 soldiers, helped to end slavery in the United States, restored the Union and strengthened the role of the Federal government.

Burley left his native land for America at the age of 21 sometime in the summer of 1861, he claimed it was in the spirit of grand adventure, but others talked of the promise of large rewards from blockade running, or pushing his fathers new invention, a submarine "torpedo" battery designed to sink a ship when attached to the hull, an idea which his father Robert had previously submitted to the British Admiralty in the 1820's, but it was rejected as it seemed far too revolutionary an idea for the time. This invention was immortalised in Jules Verne's "20000 Leagues Under the Sea", in which an underwater gun firing mechanism is described as having been perfected in England by Philip Coles and Burley.

However, a family story blames Burleys real reason for leaving on a pregnant house keeper, and/or an unblessed marriage in Glasgow to what was believed to be his housekeeper. His furious father tried to have the marriage annulled and Bennet was sent to America in disgrace. The truth of the matter is he did have a child, Marion Burley on 22nd February 1861, and a month later married the 18 year old mother Marion Thomson. Then for some reason, probably financial, despite the relationship seeming to continue for many further years he headed to the United States.

In 1861, after landing in New York, Burley approached the Federal Government, who never considered his plans as they were overrun with torpedo schemes, so he then left for Richmond, where he showed his plans to the Confederate Naval Secretary, who decided to throw him into prison as a possible spy. Its is suggested that Burley was no stranger to prison before he got to America; However the brown haired, blue eyed, barefaced adventurer was regarded with suspicion by the Confederate authorities, and had to spend several weeks in the city's Castle Thunder; he could have been hung as a union infiltrator, but saved himself by volunteering, along with a fellow Scot called John Maxwell, for the Confederate States Navy "Volunteer Coast Guard", which was a special designation shielding quasi-privateering under the official navy. The volunteer aspect was designed to enable men who couldn't be conscripted officially to the Confederacy to be used by some means; Burley took this route as he was a neutral British Citizen. It is noted that Burley himself found slavery abominable. However the two men were first given menial jobs at the Richmond Station to ensure their loyalty.

Some time later, Burley was recalled and given the opportunity to build the torpedo, and he and Maxwell succeeded in fastening it to a Union war vessel, but the fuse didn't ignite, and no damage was done. The torpedo, or "curious infernal machine" as reported by the New York Herald, was discovered still stuck to the side of the ship in New York, and was then exhibited at the corner of Fulton and Nassau, Manhattan. This account came from Judge Lucas, a friend of Burleys future officer Beall, and he probably got his accounts of Burley's adventures from Burley himself.

On September 11th 1863, Burley was promoted to Acting Master within the Navy, and served under Ned Lee, a nephew of Robert E. Lee and the University of Virginia political economy graduate John Yates Beall; Beall had been injured early in the war, and during his convalescence, approached the Southern authorities about privateering in the Chesapeake Bay area; feeling that this type of work suited him better than getting involved in sustained campaigns. The expedition was a mixed venture of both private enterprise and legal expediency. Beall was empowered to accept enlistments and draw gear from the Navy, yet he and his guerrilla band wore no uniforms, were required to procure their own sea vehicles and pay their own wages out of the prizes and cargoes that they might capture. Their base of operations loosely centred around Matthews County on the Virginian peninsula between Mobjack

Bay and the Piankatank River. Come April 1863, this band of a ten or so men set out without boats in order to cause chaos in the Chesapeake Bay Area, specializing in sabotage operations and blockade running.

This merry band accomplished little in the first few months apart from dispersing a camp of former armed slaves on the Black River, 10 miles from Fort Monroe, one man was killed, another captured and the rest ran off, but Beall's men gained a much larger arsenal. In July they crossed Chesapeake Bay and cut the cable linking Fort Monroe to Washington. In August the gang destroyed the Federal Cape Charles Lighthouse on Smith Island, taking its lamps, reflectors and a highly valuable 25 barrels (300 gallons) of sperm oil back to Richmond.

Bealls gang soon comprised about 20 men, who after commandeering a 22 foot white-hulled sailing yawl which they called the Swan, and a 28 foot black sailing canoe, called the Raven were ready to hit the shipping lanes proper.

One of the new members of the crew was W.W.Baker, an apprentice with the Richmond Enquirer Newspaper, and also on board was his boss, the Editor George Stedman. Burleigh later spent some time working at the paper, and one wonders whether it was Burleys 'campfire' conversations with these men that first gave him the idea of a future career in journalism.

On 17th September 1863, the raiders put out from Horn Harbour, and captured the sloop Mary Anne and some fishing scows off Raccoon Island, enjoying a wonderful fish supper that evening. After two days sailing up the Atlantic coast, the gang attacked the schooner Alliance in the Wachapreague inlet. The Alliance was a large supply sloop carrying some $200,000 worth of supplies for the Federal garrison at Port Royal, South Carolina. The attack took place during a fierce equatorial storm, and after a lot of trouble boarding the ship in the rough seas, they managed to surprise the crew as none had been on deck, and took the Alliance without firing a shot. From the sloops stores they all "had a veritable feast of good things, as there appeared to be everything to eat, drink, smoke and wear aboard".

The next morning, after leaving a guard on the Alliance, the men captured the Schooner J. J. Houseman, and in the evening they caught two more schooners, the Samuel Pearsall and Alexandria. Within four days and in foul weather the men had captured 7 boats, but unfortunately for Beall and his men, all the prizes had to be stripped and sent to sea as derelicts (though some were later picked up and restored by blockade runners).

The men then tried to sail the Alliance and her valuable cargo through to Richmond, but feeling threatened by a nearby Federal blockading gun boat, they were forced to ground and burn her on the bar off Milford Haven, Virginia. However they still managed to salvage and carry over $10,000 worth of goods to Richmond, enjoying ten days active rest before departing once again for Matthews county.

By October, this band of men had become a huge thorn in the Unions side, and presuming their accomplishments had been undertaken by a large number of men, the entire 4th U.S. Coloured Infantry, and regiments of Pennsylvania and New York cavalry and light artillery detachments were ordered to set up a dragnet across Matthews County .The Navy were also involved, with the USS Commodore Jones, USS Putnam, USS Stepping Stones, and 4 other army gunboats sent to watch the waterways and seal off any avenues of escape, In total about 500 men were sent to capture them. However, the gang avoided the Federal lines and laid low in a place called Dragon Swamp for three days until the troops had returned to Fort Monroe. In the meantime, a local man was hanged by the Federals for his aiding and abetting of the men; after this murder, the guerrillas of the Chesapeake were more determined than ever to injure the Federals as much as possible.

The gang then dispersed for a while until the heat died down, Burley went to Virginia City where he was forced to stay for a while, being sick with malarial fever; it was here he undertook his first literary work for the Southern Illustrated News, and made an appearance on stage in D'Orsay Ogden's production of "The Guerrilla".

Beall was determined to capture a Federal gunboat, and so on November 14th, the gang, minus the sick Burley, entered the Tangier Inlet in the Swan and Raven and captured a federal schooner. Beall remained on board and the rest of the men were ordered to find concealment until the next night; they rested up in what they thought was an excellent hidden cove, but turned out to be just the opposite. At midday, they were challenged by a local fisherman, and the Federal army turned up soon after and rounded up all the men. Beall could have escaped but held on a while as he thought he might be able to save his men. The men were briefly held in a local jail before being moved to Fort McHenry, where Beall and some 20 others were kept in close confinement and manacled with heavy irons. The Confederates soon placed the same number of Federal soldiers in close confinement and several months later, an exchange of prisoners was granted. In the meantime however, the Federal Secretary of War Stanton, wrote that the captured men would "be held for the present, not as prisoners of war but as pirates or marauding robbers". Beall was to later write of these exploits and say, "I do not know that we ever accomplished any great things . . . but we devilled the life out of the gun boats of the Chesapeake trying to catch us." The men returned to Richmond to a hero's welcome.

Come 1864, Burley became a guerrilla of the Chesapeake once again. At one 4am raid on the Cherrystone Inlet telegraph office, the gang crossed the bay in open boats, and destroyed stores, and a guard-house, along with the telegraph instruments and apparatus; they also killed and wounded 8 horses. Two Federal vessels lay at anchor two miles offshore, and made the mistake of heading for the wharf, the first steamer Aeolus was quickly captured, the captain being robbed of $3000 and the boat later destroyed. In the meantime, the steam-tug Titan approached, was captured, and then used by the raiders for their escape, taking 19 prisoners with them. The gang were chased up the Piankatank River, but the Federals halted as they did not know the rivers course. The gang seized the sugar, coffee and whisky from the Titan and disappeared; the Federals found the boat burnt out the following morning. The Captain of the expedition, Fitzhugh said Burley acted gallantly and was of great value to the success of the expedition. The flag of the Titan is now in the public library in Richmond. Burley was also credited in 1864, for the destruction of the Bowlers Rock Lightship that lay on the Rappahannock River between Bowlers Landing and Suggetts Point.

On March 30th, 1864, Burley, Maxwell and Daniel Lucas received a pass to go to Libby Prison in Richmond, authorising them to interrogate Federal prisoners who had been captured on the Eastern Shore of Virginia. Soon after, on May 12th 1864, a Federal coloured infantry, after a sharp fight, captured Burley and his comrades whilst they were laying torpedoes at Stingray Point, Virginia. Some of the men were killed, Burley was shot and injured, but the papers on his person - a British protection, and a pass dated March 30, 1864, that allowed him to pass beyond the limits of the Confederate States exposed him to the suspicion that he was a spy. The men were lucky, as the Federal Colonel noted in his report, that all the men would have been killed, were it not for the restraint of his sergeant. The Colonel described the nine torpedoes they discovered and destroyed, as being "constructed with tin cases, each containing about 50 pounds of powder".

FORT DELAWARE

      The captured men were taken to Fort Delaware, a prison which lies on a small island some forty miles below Philadelphia. On July 1st Burley and some comrades attempted to escape through the forts sewage system which ran under the cells and into the Delaware river. The water in the sewers came up to the sleepers on which the cell floor rested. Burley managed to pry up several planks, and along with five others, crawled through the opening. For 125 yards they crawled through the sewer, diving under sleepers as they came to them, but the tide nearly made this impossible. At the mouth of the sewer, two men were recaptured and two others drowned in the river. Burleigh and another man swam for five hours in the darkness; the distance to land is actually only about a mile and a half, but the river is very cold and runs at 3 knots; they were very lucky men to survive. However, survival was not impossible for the very fit, as in modern times there is a triathlon swim out to the island. What happened next is somewhat of a mystery, some say they landed in Salem, New Jersey, which was enemy territory, dressed in Confederate grey. The official story, indicates that mid river, the men convinced a boats captain that they were capsized fishermen, and so his ship then dropped them off in Philadelphia from where they made their way to freedom in Canada. Perhaps a more likely story is that there may have been a boat waiting to spirit the men away, or that they happened across some allies, the area being full of Confederate sympathisers, with nearby Baltimore being the most northern "Southern City". Another version of this story suggests that Burley swam to a British ship anchored in the river, and convinced the captain he had fallen overboard a departing vessel, had no military connections, and was a British subject returning to Canada. In later life, Burleigh never publicly discuss his exploits during the American Civil War, however, he did discuss them privately, and was very proud of moments such as this, despite the expense of losing most of the skin on his back as he wriggled to freedom.

Part B - Guerrillas on Lake Erie.

In February 1864, the Confederate Congress passed a bill that authorized a campaign of sabotage against "the enemy's property, by land or sea."; and a fund of $1 million was earmarked for use by agents in Canada then known as British North America; Britain's "neutrality" favoured the South and King Cotton. In March, Captain Hines, who had ridden in guerrilla sorties with General Morgan in Kentucky and Tennessee, where he had made contacts with leaders of pro-South underground networks was briefed amongst other things, to arrange passage for soldiers to return to the Confederate army lines, and also to effect " any fair and appropriate enterprises of war against our enemies … {meeting} neutral obligations incumbent in the British Provinces". Shortly after Hines reached Canada, Jacob Thompson, the Special Commissioner of the Confederate States Government in Canada arrived to direct and oversee operations. Before resorting to more extreme measures he sought to negotiate with northerners who might "be relied upon to aid the attainment of peace". He hoped to use those who wanted peace to force their ideals on the administration; he also aimed to raise a more forceful insurrection in the Northwest states (now the Midwest) against the Union, and bring an end to the war on Southern terms. An estimated 40 percent of the Midwest population was Southern-born and many belonged to secret societies, such as the Knights of the Golden Circle or the Order of the Sons of Liberty (300,000 members claimed), who wore the head of Liberty, cut from copper pennies on their lapels (their enemies thus calling them Copperheads). However the plan failed generally as the men who were asked to aid the Confederates (about 500) were citizens who were hostile to the war but not particularly loyal to the confederacy.

When Beall was about to begin his operations around the Canadian border, he reported to Thompson, and was delighted to be invited to command an enterprise similar to his own ideas of freeing the Confederate prisoners on Johnson's Island. He immediately began to scout for recruits and unexpectedly bumped into Burley whilst walking the streets of Toronto.

Not far from the Canadian border lay two large Union prisoner of war camps— Fort Douglas in Chicago and Johnson's Island, near Sandusky, Ohio; the prisoners on this island, who lived in terrible conditions, consisted mainly of a large number of seasoned Confederate officers who had been captured at Vicksburg and Port Hudson. In order to enlist these soldiers for a general insurrection in the north west, the conspirators came up with an elaborate plan: their agents would slip out of Canada, take over Lake Erie river steamers, and use them as impromptu warships for the boarding and seizure of the U.S.S. Michigan, which was the only ship guarding this vast lake for the Union. The Michigan was the pride of the Union Navy, built in 1844, it was their first iron hulled ship, a side wheeled steamboat with three sailing masts. The boat was 163 feet long and 25 feet wide; this formidable craft carried a 60 pound cannon and 14 twelve pound cannons. The Confederates would then use it to attack Johnson's Island in order to free and arm the two to three thousand prisoners imprisoned there. In coordinated raids, prisoners at Fort Douglas would also be freed and armed. The Confederate soldiers, allied with the Sons of Liberty, would then open up a new confederate heartland in the region, whilst using the U.S.S. Michigan to rain destruction on cities along the Great Lakes, thus forcing the Union to look for peace. The Confederacy had initially looked at capturing the Michigan as early as February 1863, and whilst the heads of the Confederate Navies and Armies loved the plan, President Davis feared it might upset the neutrality and the official recognition of the Confederacy by Great Britain, and thus interfere with the production of the ironclad rams the British were supplying.

Burley was one of the men charged with releasing the prisoners on Johnsons Island, the resulting events of which would become known as the Philo Parsons affair, his most famous exploit of the Civil War. The plot was finalised in the Ontario home of Burleys cousin and Confederate sympathizer, Adam Robertson, a Scotsman who had moved to Guelph in 1847. Robertson had helped established two iron foundries in Guelph, one in partnership with the Inglis family, who would later gain fame as appliance manufacturers, before starting his own factory in 1852, on Eramosa Road, not far from the house he built on Mitchell Street. Robertson would eventually become the towns Mayor; he was highly regarded as a respected employer. Although the manufacturing of farm implements were the factories main stock-in-trade, they also made a few cannon, cannonballs and grenades for the Confederacy. According to Professor Stelter, of Guelph University, who lived in the Robertson's home and found copies of correspondence written by the conspirators, he said it was common knowledge in Guelph that the foundry was turning out more than ploughs and harrows. The men there were also experimenting with Greek Fire in order to attempt to burn down New York

City; this attempt to terrorise the city failed due to the products unreliability. One of the foundries cannon remains overlooking Vancouver's Horseshoe Bay. According to Robertson's son (speaking in 1917), the conspirators planned to ship munitions to Lake Erie where they would be used to free Confederate prisoners. The plot follows thus: In July 1864 Captain Cole (a genial banker by day), was sent to the Great Lakes area to scout out the possibility of capturing the steamer Michigan. At first he thought he might just be able to purchase a steamer in Toronto and outfit it with the cannon cast in Robertson's foundry. However, the decision was taken to capture a steamer by force.

Captain Beall and his men were going to have to rely on surprise, revolvers and knives to capture the Michigan. A cannon-shot was then to be sent through the prisoners quarters on the island to signify that the hour for their release had come as it had been previously ascertained from the escaped prisoners of Johnson's Island that an organization existed amongst the inmates that someday planned to surprise the guard and capture the island. The prisoners assistant quartermaster, Archibald McKennon, wrote, "We were organised into companies and regiments and had armed ourselves with clubs …in constant expectation of orders … to make the fight." The "officers" had had several conferences with the colonel of the organization as to duties, and were constantly expecting orders to fight, but they never came. One soldier reminisced, "It surely would have been a pitiable affair, for the undertaking was wholly impracticable".

On the evening of Sunday September 18th 1864, whilst the Philo Parsons was docked in Detroit, Burley approached Clerk Ashley, part owner of the ship, and asked for him by name. Burley was described as "a thick-set young man of about 25, with a strange accent, evidently Scotch or English and dressed in English clothes. A little below the medium height, he had sandy hair and a thin beard to go with "the bearing of a gentleman"". Burley told Ashley that he and a party of friends were planning a pleasure trip the following day, and asked Ashley whether he could go slightly off his regular course and stop at Sandwich, on the Canadian side, so his friends could get on board, as one of them was lame. Ashley agreed so long as Burley himself joined the boat at Detroit, so he would be sure that his friends were ready. The Philo Parsons was a wooden hulled, side wheel steamboat, 135 foot long and 22 feet wide, weighing 22 tons.

At 8am on Monday morning, on what was remembered as a lovely day, Burley boarded, and later at Sandwich, his three companions, dressed as civilians, got on board, one of whom was Beall, whose lameness shortly disappeared. When the boat arrived at the later port of Amhertsburg, another 16 men boarded and were presumed to be returning American draft dodgers, which was not considered unusual. They carried one trunk, secretly containing arms. The two groups seemed to have no connection, and nothing unusual was noted. Burley was reportedly most attentive to the ladies on board, turning the pages for those who played the piano, singing songs and chatting freely, as well as attending to their comfort on deck. At about four o'clock in the afternoon, Beall, who had been talking with the mate at the wheel, drew a pistol and declared that as a Confederate officer he was taking possession of the steamer and seizing the boat. At the same time three others levelled revolvers at Ashley, and Burley with pistol ready said "Get into that cabin, or you are a dead man . . . One ... two ... "; he didn't have to count to three, as Ashley quickly joined the other 50 or so passengers with a guard being placed at the door. Soon enough, the old trunk was opened and hatchets and revolvers were passed out to the whole party. The gang soon were in control of the Parsons. Burley took charge of the deck and, because Ashley had not given him the keys, he said he would make a key, and proceeded to axe down the baggage doors and throw overboard the deck load, consisting of iron, household goods, and tobacco; perhaps this led to Burley later being described by passengers as a "perfect desperado". It must be noted at this point that the descriptions of Burley throughout his career are widely different, the kind of character you would either love or hate. He and Beall then took Ashley to his office and compelled him to give up the steamer's papers. These events occurred between four and five o'clock in the afternoon, and lasted for several hours.

During this time, the boat had run down the lake to a point from which the ships mate, Nicholls, later testified that the Michigan was plainly visible in Sandusky Bay. The conspirators asked Nicholls many questions about the Michigan and Parsons, and when it was learned from him that the Parsons was low on fuel, he was ordered to turn her about and head for Middle Bass Island, where wood could be taken on board. Whilst the Parsons was still loading up and lying at the wharf, another boat, the Island Queen came alongside, having on board about twenty-five unarmed Union soldiers from the 130th Ohio Infantry, who were on their way to Toledo to be mustered out; the rebel gang made a rush to board her, firing their pistols and injuring the engineer with a shot to the face. These Federal soldiers were the most northerly capture by the Confederates during the whole Civil War. The passengers were eventually put ashore. Just before the rebels put Ashley ashore, Beall and Burley took the ships money - about $10, Burley then threatened Ashley, "You have more money, and let us have it", at which point he took about $100 from his jacket pocket. Ashley says that the two men then split the money between them. The landed soldiers were paroled not to bear arms against the Confederacy until regularly exchanged, and the civilians were required to promise that they would say nothing of what had happened for twenty- four hours. The two steamers were then lashed together and five miles away on Chickanolee Reef, the Island Queen was scuttled. There are two other versions of what happened to the Island Queen, firstly that its passengers tried to board the Parsons, but were driven back, but it seems more likely that they boarded her to tie on to as she was blocking the dock, and they were thus captured; another version has the captain of the Parsons, who had been dropped off earlier at his home on the island, arriving just as the fight broke out, only to be captured and put in the hold.

As the night wore on, the rebel crew grew suspicious and apprehensive due to a failure to receive the all clear message at Kelly's Island from Captain Cole, their man in Sandusky. Although it is noted that another man joined the crew at Kelly's Island; he perhaps reported that he had not received the all clear message he had been waiting for. It was now after midnight, the night was clear and moonlit, and the men could see through their glasses that the Michigan had taken up a position commanding the whole of Johnsons Island and thus believed that the enemy was aware of their approach which frightened them a little. The rebels briefly considered using the element of surprise and ramming the Michigan but felt its guns could finish them off before they got close. However, they reverted to the original plan, later described by a Captain Hunter; in which the Confederates would set fire to the Parsons at the entrance of Sandusky Bay, causing the crew of the Michigan to launch a rescue mission for supposed passengers, allowing the conspirators to get the upper hand on their saviours and thus gain the deck of the warship without arousing suspicion. A watchman did report the making of three combustible balls on board whilst the ship was under Bealls command, but they were probably to be used for burning down the house of a local banker whom they intended to rob, or the Parsons when she was abandoned.

However, due to the mens fear, they threatened mutiny, so an apparently furious Beall abandoned the plan, requiring that the "mutineers" sign a written statement, which was drawn up on the back of a bill of loading; It read: "On Board the Philo Parsons, September 20, 1864 - We the undersigned crew of the boat aforesaid, take pleasure in expressing our admiration of the gentlemanly bearing skill and courage of Captain Beall as a commanding officer and a gentleman, but believing and being well convinced that the enemy is informed of our approach, and is so well prepared that we cannot possibly make it a success, and having already captured two boats, we respectfully decline to prosecute it any further". This document was signed by 17 men; Burley was not one of them. With great reluctance on the part of Beall, the boat was turned back toward the Detroit River, and the residents of Middle Bass Island who were out burying their valuables, saw her steaming by in the darkness with the Confederate flag fluttering on her mast. There was also some talk of attacking a vessel or two that they passed, and of robbing the island home of a Detroit banker named Ives. The Parsons plunder was landed near Malden, and she was then abandoned at Sandwich; some of her furniture being put ashore and her injection pipes cut, so that she would fill and sink. The raiders then disappeared, a couple of them who were later arrested by the Canadian authorities were discharged by a Justice of the Peace after a detention of two hours. The Parsons was later lost in the Great Fire of Chicago, and the Michigan's hull now serves as a monument at Erie. Right up until his death, Beall believed that, without the mutiny, the men could have captured the Michigan with certainty, and that the later stories of the betrayal and /or the capture of their man on shore were simply fabricated in order to cover up the gross dereliction of duty by both the mutineers and the officers of the Michigan.

The Confederates plan had relied on Captain Cole, their man on shore, to ingratiate himself with the local military authorities by posing as a wealthy oil tycoon. On the night of the raid, Cole had invited the officers of the Michigan to a banquet in the local town of Sandusky, during which he planned to poison them, and then send a signal rocket to inform Captain Beall that the officers were absent, but the signal never reached the Parsons causing its crew to decide that the game was up and disappear to Canada. This signal was also meant to indicate to the prisoners on Johnsons Island that they should ready themselves for an uprising and upon escape head for the Federal arsenal at Sandusky. Union records show that Cole had in fact been arrested after a tip off from a Confederate prisoner held aboard the Michigan who had "disclosed the whole plot" in time for the Union warship to prepare for battle.

Two days before the Parsons was boarded, a man professing to be a Confederate refugee called at the Union headquarters in Detroit and gave a tip off leading to the following telegram being sent to the Michigan's commander Captain Carter :

DETROIT, September 17, 1864.

It is reported to me that some of the officers and men of your steamer have been tampered with, and that a party of rebel refugees leave Windsor tomorrow with the expectation of getting possession of your steamer. Signed; BH Hill Lieutenant-Colonel U. S. Army, Military Commander.

The informant can possibly be identified as Mr Smith, also known as Godfrey Hyams of Little Rock, Arkansas, a close confidant of the Canadian Confederates, and a former Confederate who kept a Windsor hotel frequented by Southerners, and who had, on other occasions supplied the Federal authorities with information, Whoever he was, he visited Lieutenant-Colonel Hill again on the Sunday with such further facts that another telegram was sent on the Monday :

DETROIT, September 19, 1864.
Capt J. C. CARTER, U. S. Navy :
It is said the parties will embark to-day at Malden on board the Philo Parsons, and will seize either that steamer or another running from Kelly's Island. Since my last despatch, I am again assured that officers and men have been bought by a man named Cole; a few men to be introduced on board under guise of friends of officers; an officer named Eddy to be drugged. Both Commodore Gardner and myself look upon the matter as serious.
B. H. Hill. Lieutenant-Col U. S. Army Acting Asst Provost Marshal General.

As Cole had intended to have some of the Michigan's officers ashore at a party that evening there was perhaps some basis for the talk of drugged wine. A Captain Hunter remembered two previous occasions when Cole had sent wine to the officers of the Michigan. Lieutenant-Colonel Hill visited the Parsons on the Monday morning and decided that it was too small if taken to be a threat, and if there was a plot, he decided to let it proceed, in order to effect the capture of the conspirators; besides this, there had been many rumours over the previous year about a raid from Canada, but nothing had come of the talk, and as no time, date or individual had been named, this too was thought to be just another scare.

Captain Carter of the Michigan, soon replied to the first telegraph stating that he was ready, and that the report of treachery on board the Michigan must be unfounded, and on receiving the second telegram, he vouched for all the crew except perhaps one steward.

Captain Hunter was sent to arrest Cole at about 3pm and found him at the West House Hotel with a woman; he had paid his bill and was seemingly about to leave Sandusky. Hunter, acting friendly with Cole, told him that he should go to the Michigan and confirm the officers attendance at that evenings dinner party with his superiors. Cole assented and ordered the inevitable drinks, but Hunter, mindful of the despatch about being drugged, made an excuse to avoid swallowing any whiskey until he had seen Cole drink out of the same bottle.

On the way to the boat, Hunter and Cole stopped off at a bank, where Cole drew out $900 in gold. When the men finally reached the wharf, Hunter pushed Cole into the Michigan's landing boat much to Coles annoyance, and Hunter told him that he was now a prisoner. The arrest being managed in this way in order to avoid alarming any of Cole's accomplices. On boarding the ship Cole was taken to the commander, who held a revolver to his head while Hunter searched him, finding among his papers his commission as a major in a Tennessee regiment. Upon Cole's admissions seven arrests were made in Sandusky. A keen watch was kept all night for the Parsons but nothing was seen. It was thought that two days of wood had been loaded at Middle Bass Island, and that the men of the Parsons may have disappeared for reinforcements and weapons, or with the plot having been foiled they were about to commit other depredations on the lake anyway. The following morning, the Michigan got under way and proceeded to Middle Bass Island, but there was nobody to take her line until the huge form of her 300 pound pilot, who was widely recognized, assured them that she was not in rebel hands. Clerk Ashley and one of John Brown's sons, who had left his island home in a rowboat to carry the news to Sandusky, were picked up, but nothing could be learned of the Parsons, and the Michigan turned back. It gave considerable relief when the Michigan entered Sandusky Bay and her officers saw the stars and stripes still waving over

Johnson's Island. In the summer of 1865 an officer of the Department of Justice made a report on Cole's case, the gist of which was that while he was plainly guilty of several offences, the least of which was a breach of his parole, there were serious difficulties in the way of his conviction and involvement in the plot, and he was consequently released in February, 1866.

If the capture of Johnson Island had been successful, it was expected that the Sons of Liberty would have aided the escaped prisoners; Thompson wrote, " Should they take the island, boats were to be improvised and Sandusky was to be attacked. If taken, the prisoners were to be mounted and make for Cleveland, the boats cooperating; and from Cleveland the prisoners were to make for Wheeling and thence to Virginia". The rebels presence on Lake Erie had not been a complete failure for the Confederacy; the people of the cities located on the Great Lakes were in a state of panic which caused the Federals to deploy troops there which were much needed elsewhere.

After the Lake Erie raid, Burley returned to his cousins house in Guelph, and a month into his return another plot was hatched as this letter from Burley shows:

GUELPH [ONTARIO, CANADA],
October 17, 1864.
DEAR SIR: Everything is going ahead finely, and I anticipate having the things finished early, perhaps this week; anyhow in the fore part of next. Probably I will be in Toronto on Wednesday. Be about, so that I can run you off down here; and I presume you will like this place. Has Colonel T. [Thompson] been able to procure the article? What about the G. F. [Greek fire] I forgot to ask you if the composition does not require some time to saturate before it can be used. Inform. Please also send me a dozen of the finest waterproof caps along with Mr. McDonald's parcel. They are for the troops. Mr. M. will likely acquaint you that an alteration has been made in the Gren [sic] [grenade] form. I will show you a pattern when we meet.

Sincerely, yours,
BENNETT BURLEY.
Dr. S. B. [JAMES T.] RATES,
Toronto.
Address just Adam Robertson, Foundry, Guelph.

Greek Fire was similar to our modern napalm, it would adhere to surfaces, ignite upon contact, and water alone would not extinguish its flames, devastation was likely. Late in October, after the disappointment of the Philo Parsons affair, the rebels purchased the steamer Georgian in Toronto and hoped to fit it out with the cannon and a ram cast in Robertson's foundry in order to attack and sink the Michigan and then use it against federal commerce and cities on the lakes; however, The boat and Burley were seized by the authorities before the plot could commence.

Part C - Arrest and Extradition

After the Philo Parsons affair, both Beall and Burley had rewards placed upon their heads. Beall was arrested and later hanged in New York for treason. Burley was captured by the Canadians in Toronto on December 3rd 1864 (who thought at first that they had captured Beall) and faced extradition to the US. His extradition was ordered on a technical charge of robbery, but the United States did not venture for the more serious charge of piracy, because there was a technical question of whether piracy could be committed on Lake Erie, which was due to the fact that until then Great Britain had ruled the waves for many years, and only recognised piracy as a crime being committed on salt water, rather than fresh. Popular sentiment in Canada, had at first been in favour of the North, but now the people had a great deal of sympathy for the Southern cause. Therefore, there were divergent views of Burley as a British hero risking his life in a noble cause, or Burley as a mere adventurer or pirate who had violated Canadian neutrality.

In the Toronto police court the warrant for Burleys arrest was found to be defective, and he was released, only to be immediately rearrested on a second warrant, and then being discharged once again upon habeas corpus hearings (a writ requiring a person to be brought before a judge or into court and a jury of his peers, especially to investigate the lawfulness of their detention). While Burley was delayed in the courtroom receiving congratulations from his admirers, he was served with a third warrant, and this time it was in proper form, issued by a proper authority, and he was immediately taken before the Recorder for a hearing on the application for extradition, which was granted.

At the prisoner's request, a month delay was granted by the Recorder so as to enable Burley to obtain proof from Richmond that he was acting under authority of the Confederate Government. A messenger was thence despatched, on a dangerous mission through Federal lines; and when trial resumed, the defence was able to produce Burley's commission as Acting Master in the Confederate Navy, and also the special message signed by President Davis himself.

The above journey of the above messenger, Lt. Davis, provides another harrowing story. On his journey from Toronto to Richmond, he was arrested in Newark, Ohio, tried before a court-martial as a spy, and sentenced to death. He was incarcerated at Johnson's Island, and had given up hope, when, on the day of his execution, he was sent under guard to Fort Delaware to serve imprisonment instead of forfeiting his life. A letter written by Jacob Thompson, the Special Commissioner of the Confederate States Government in Canada, to President Lincoln may have helped this prisoner in his hour of need:

Toronto, Canada, February 2nd 1865.
To his Excellency, A. Lincoln, President of the United States:

    Sir - The telegraph announces that Lt. S. B. Davies identified in Newark, Ohio, confessed, on his arrest, to being the bearer of important despatches from Richmond to Canada, has been sentenced to be hung at Johnson's Island on the 17th of February. Another paper states that Lt. Davies has been condemned as a spy. This young man's life is in your hands, and I hope you will allow me to discharge a duty I owe to you, to myself, to Lt. Davies, to justice, and to humanity, to demonstrate fully the facts in the case, so far as they are known to me, upon honour. Lt. Davies is a citizen of the state of Delaware, and has been for some time an officer in the Confederate service. No braver or truer soldier can be found in either army. He is a gentleman of education, true in all his transactions, and beloved and respected by all who know him. In the trial of Acting Master Bennet G. Burley, a case for extradition, the Recorder at Toronto has postponed the investigation for 30 days to enable the accused to obtain certain documentary evidence being important to his defence, from Richmond. The government at Richmond was duly informed of this. Mr Burley's counsel deemed these documents essential, and Lt. Davies volunteered to bring them to Canada. As he was pressed for time, he came direct through the United States and reached here in six days, which was regarded a most expeditious trip. It was impossible for him on this trip to have acted the spy in any sense of that term. He remained here but three days in all. Lt Davies was directed to return by the most certain route to Richmond, with the quickest possible despatch, in order that the authorities might furnish the documents asked for by the counsel of the accused. The whole object and aim of his coming here was to obtain the proofs deemed necessary to secure the administering of justice to his former companion in arms.

    As I received the despatches he brought and wrote those he carried, I know every word in them, and as every word related to the case then undergoing judicial investigation, there could have been no objection to your reading them; hence I know that, however much you may desire to crush out the Confederate States Government, it must be repugnant to your sense of right and justice and humanity to pursue individuals with unnecessary harshness. When Lt. Davies was arrested he was on the very route he had advised me he would take in order to avoid all contact with the military authorities. He was expecting to gain no information with respect to the movement of your armies, nor do I believe he sought to do so. As a private citizen, speaking to one clothed with authority, I ask you to spare this young man's life, not from any favour to me, but for the sake of justice, humanity, and all the conditions which control intercourse between hostile people. You have the right to retain him as a prisoner of war, but I declare on honour he is not a spy.

Very respectfully yours,
(Signed) Jacob Thompson.

Several months after his arrest, Burleys trial took place, and the Toronto Globe of January 28, 1865, published the following arguments and judgements of the court, presented here in edited form. The newspapers editorial stated that the Court was very crowded, chiefly by the friends of the prisoner and a strong force of police in attendance. The prisoner was seated in the body of the court, well protected by guards.

At the trial, Burley was accused that on the 19th of September, 1864, "on board the "Philo Parsons", a vessel belonging in whole or part to Walter O. Ashley, a citizen of the United States, such vessel being then upon the high seas, ... feloniously made an assault on the said Ashley, and feloniously put him in bodily fear and danger of his life, and one promissory note issued by the Secretary of the Treasury of the United States of the denomination and value of $20, and in general use as currency, and being the property of the said Ashley and other persons, from the person and against the will of the said Ashley feloniously did steal and rob etc, contrary to the Act of Congress, approved at April 30, 1719, commonly called the Piracy Act."

Arguments raged that the crime, if tried in the Erie County Court in the State of Ohio, would be robbery, but if tried in Detroit it would be the crime of robbery on the lakes, in other words, piracy within the territory of United States.

On behalf of the prisoner, evidence was given that in February and March 1864, he was seen in Richmond, in Confederate uniform, wearing a badge of military rank. He was also in Richmond in May 1863. It was proved that he was born either at Greenock or Glasgow, in Scotland. He was in Canada about the beginning of August 1864, and also in the month of October following. He had been a prisoner of war in a fort belonging to the United States, and had escaped. It was also proved that the 15 acre site of Johnson's Island was a military prison of United States, and that there are about 2600 prisoners there, consisting principally of Confederate officers - enough men to lead 80,000 troops. The witness (Robert Kennedy) stated that he had been a captain in the Confederate States, and had escaped from prison, and he was aware that an attempt was to be made sometime in September last to release the prisoners; that there is also a Federal military force on the island, and a gunboat called the "Michigan". That Burleigh was in uniform when taken, and was treated, not as a rebel, but as a prisoner of war. Evidence was also adduced to prove the authenticity of the follow three documents, which were received by the Recorder.

1. *"Confederate States of America, Navy Department, Richmond. September 11, 1863"*

"Sir, You are hereby informed that the President has appointed you an Acting Master in the navy of the Confederate States. You are requested to signify your acceptance or non-acceptance of the appointment; and should you accept, you are to sign, before a Magistrate, the oath of office herewith forwarded, and forward the same with your letter of acceptance to this Department. Registered No.
　　　　The lowest number takes rank."
　　　　　　(Signed)　　　"S.R. MALLORY, *Secretary of the Navy.*

"Acting Master Bennet G. Burley
Confederate States Navy, Richmond, Va."

To this document was added the following endorsement:-

Confederate States of America, Richmond, December 22, 1864.

2. I certify that the reverse of this page presents a true copy of the warrant granted to Bennett G. Burley, as an Acting Master in the navy of the Confederate States, from the records of this Department.
　　　　In testimony whereof I have hereunto set my hand and affixed the

seal of this Department, on the day and year above written.

    (L.S.)   (Signed)   "S.R. MALLORY, *Secretary of the Navy*" *Confederate States of America*

    3. Whereas it has been made known to me that Bennett G. Burley, an Acting Master in the navy of the Confederate States, is now under arrest in one of the British North American Provinces, on an application made by the Government of the United States for the delivery to that Government of the said Bennett G. Burley, under the Treaty known as the Extradition Treaty, now in force between the United States and Great Britain; and whereas it has been represented to me that the demand for the extradition of the said Bennet G. Burley is based on the charge that the said Burley is a fugitive from justice, charged with having committed crimes of robbery and piracy in the jurisdiction of the United States; and whereas it has further been made known to me that the accusations and charges made against the said Bennett G. Burley, are based solely on the acts and conduct of the said Burley in an enterprise or expedition for the capture of the said armed steamer "Michigan", an armed vessel of the United States, navigating the lakes on the boundary between the United States and the British American Provinces, and for the release of numerous citizens of the Confederate States, held as prisoners of war by the United States at a certain Island called Johnson's Island; and whereas the said enterprise or expedition for the capture of the said armed steamer "Michigan", and for the release of the said prisoners on Johnson's Island, was a proper and legitimate belligerent operation, undertaken during the pending public war between the two Confederacies, known respectively as the Confederate States of America and the United States of America, which operation was ordered and sanctioned by the authority of the Government of the Confederate States, and confided to its commissioned officers for execution, among which officers is the said Bennet G. Burley:

    Now, therefore, I Jefferson Davies , President of the Confederate States of America, do hereby declare and make known to all whom it may concern that the expedition aforesaid, undertaken in the month of September last, for the capture of the armed steamer Michigan, a vessel of war of the United States, and for the release of the prisoners of war, citizens of the Confederate States of America, held captive by the United States of America at Johnson's Island, was a belligerent expedition, ordered and undertaken under the authority of the Confederate States of

America, against the United states of America, and that the Government of the Confederate States of America assumes the responsibility of answering for the acts and conduct of any of its officers engaged in the said expedition, and especially of the said Bennet G. Burley, an acting master in the Navy of the Confederate States.

And I do further make known to all whom it may concern that in the orders and instructions given to the officers engaged in the said expedition they were specially directed and enjoined to "abstain from violating any of the laws and regulations of the Canadian or British authorities in relation to neutrality", and that the combination necessary to the fact that the purpose of said expedition "must be made by Confederate soldiers and such assistance as they might (you may) draw from the enemies country.

In testimony whereof, I have signed this manifesto and directed the same to be sealed with the seal of the Department of State of the Confederate States of America, and to be made public.
Done at the city of Richmond on this 24th day of September 1864.
{correct date as per document}

[SIGNED.]   JEFFERSON DAVIS

By The President:
J.P. BENJAMIN,
Secretary of State.

This remarkable document is considered of a distinct historical and legal interest, in that it had previously been presumed that once a government assumed responsibility for the act of an individual, the act became national in character, and was no longer subject to the jurisdiction of the criminal court. The result of this letter proved different, because in his anxiety to shield Burley, President Davis had protested too much - by stating that his officers had been warned against violating the neutrality of Canada, Burley had therefore disobeyed orders.

The British were also unimpressed with the letter, the Foreign and Commonwealth Office wrote on February 13th, 1865. "...the President of the so-called Confederate States has put forth a proclamation claiming as a belligerent operation on behalf of the Confederate States, the act of Bennett G. Burley in attempting in 1864 to capture the steamer

"Michigan" with a view to release numerous prisoners detained in captivity on Johnson's Island, in Lake Erie. Independently of this proclamation, the facts connected with the attack on other American steamers, the "Philo Parsons" and "Island Queen," on Lake Erie, ...show a gross disregard of Her Majesty's character as a neutral power, and a desire to involve Her Majesty in hostilities with a conterminous power with which Great Britain is at peace".

Burley's Defence objected to the sufficiency of the evidence used to justify the warrant, and the warrant itself, which they felt ought to set out the evidence upon which it was issued; in that it should show that the Governor-General authorised and directed the Recorder to take proceedings against the prisoner, and / or that proceedings against Burley originated in the United States.

At this point it is worth noting the memories of the civilian artist and engineer William Armstrong of Toronto who claims he sent a cipher to Jefferson Davis, the purpose of which was to get Burleys commission antedated in order to cover the Philo Parsons affair.

The Chief Justice judged that; "none of these objections are sustainable. The authority of the Recorder which enacts that "upon complaint made upon oath or affirmation ... charging any person found within the limits of this Province with having committed, within the jurisdiction of the United States of America ... it shall be lawful for {the Recorder) to issue his warrant for the apprehension of the party so charged, that he may be brought before him, and upon the said person being brought before him under the said warrant, it shall be lawful for such Judge, ..., to examine upon oath any person or persons touching the truth of such charge, and upon such evidence ... would justify the apprehension and committal for trial of the person so accused. {to remain in gaol } until surrendered according to the ... Treaty, or until discharged according to the law, and the Judge shall thereupon forthwith transmit or deliver to the Governor a copy of all the testimony taken before him, that a warrant may issue upon the requisition of the United States for the surrender of all such persons pursuant to the said Treaty". and that nothing in the Act required that the evidence against the accused should be noted in the warrant. He added that the text of the present writ may have errors, but that the mistakes are of no consequence".

The Chief Justice also argued that although it appeared that the prisoner was a native-born subject of Her Majesty, it didn't matter as the law covered all persons who committed crimes in the United States and who were then found in Canada.

The Chief Justice added that "It was further objected that the prisoner is proved to be an officer in the service of the Southern Confederacy - but there is an existing state of war between that Confederacy in the United States of America; that this state of war gives rise to, as between the belligerents themselves, certain rights acknowledged by the law of nations, and among them an immunity as regards all acts of hostility done either in the enemy's country or against the lives and property of the enemies subjects and citizens. That the act charged as robbery was an act done in the prosecution of lawful hostilities, and though committed within the territory of the United States, was not a crime against the municipal law of the country. That Great Britain has recognised this state of war, and has, by a declaration of neutrality, admitted the existence in each of those rights which belong to belligerents. Hence it is argued that the judicial authorities of this country cannot treat such acts as the prisoner is charged with committing, under the circumstances as appearing, as crimes such as the Extradition Treaty was intended to apply to." He added that it is established that the alleged state of war exists, but also recognises the obligations arising from the neutrality of Britain, which should be observed by the Queen's subjects towards the belligerents, and Burley, by entering military service as a belligerent is at odds with his duty as a British subject".

The Chief Justice also noted that some of Burleys comrades made inquiries and spoke of their plans in a manner indicating private pillage rather than warlike enterprise. He however conceded that "there is evidence that the prisoner was an officer in the Confederate service, and that he had the sanction of those who employed him to endeavour to capture the "Michigan", and to release the prisoners on Johnson's Island, but the manifesto put forward as a shield to protect the prisoner from personal responsibility does not extend to what he had actually done … it absolutely prohibits a violation of neutral territory or of any rights of neutrals. The prisoner, however, according to the testimony, was a leader in an expedition embarked surreptitiously from a neutral territory; his followers, with their weapons, found him in that territory, and proceeded thence to prosecute their enterprise, whatever it was, into the territory of the United States. Thus, assuming their intentions to have been what was professed, they deprived the expedition of the character of lawful hostility, and the very commencement and embarkation of their enterprise was a violation of neutral territory, and contrary to the letter and spirit of the manifesto produced. One wonders if the alleged belligerent enterprise was put forward as a pretext to cloak very different designs".

"Taken by themselves the acts of the prisoner himself clearly established a prima facie case of robbery with violence - at least according to our law. The matters alleged to deprive the prisoners acts this criminal character, are necessarily to be set up by the way of defence to the charge, and involve the admission that the prisoner committed the acts, but denting their criminality". He concluded that, "Assuming some act done within our jurisdiction, which, unexplained, would amount to robbery - if explanations were offered, and evidence to support them, were given at a preliminary investigation, the accused could not be discharged - the case must be submitted to a jury. This case cannot, from its very nature, be investigated before our tribunals, for the act was committed in the jurisdiction of the United States. Whether those facts necessary to rebut the prima facie case can be proved, can only be determined by the Courts of that country. We are bound to assume that they will try and decide it justly".

Following the judgement of the Chief Justice, Mr Justice Richards' added his opinion, and he also found no evidence that the Recorders warrant was invalid.

Mr Justice Richards then discussed another objection, in that the prisoner was charged in the United States with piracy, and that he cannot now be committed for the crime of robbery. He argued that "The charge made in this Province under which the prisoner was arrested was robbery. If the requisition on behalf of the United States Government is for his extradition for the crime of piracy, I apprehend that he could not be surrendered under the warrant of commitment before us. He may have been found guilty of the crime of piracy in the United States, but as this charge is one of robbery, the fact that he was charged with piracy there, cannot prevent his being surrendered for robbery, if such an offence is charged and proved against him here ... When this requisition is made, if his surrender is required for any offence other than the one charged against him here, and for which he is committed, as already remarked, it must be refused; and when surrendered, I apprehend that the United States Government, would in good faith, be bound to try him for the offence upon which he was surrendered."

Having expressed his opinion on most if not all of the preliminary questions, Justice Richards discussed that some of the party guarding the pilot of the Philo Parsons asked him if a banker did not live on Grosse Isle, in the Detroit River, adding that, if it had not been so late they would go and rob him. Also, they only hoisted the Confederate flag after dark, and then only half-mast. He argued that the evidence to show that the prisoner was an officer of the belligerent power, as he contended he was, was not sufficient, and that the instrument called a manifesto does not show that this prisoner was directed to engage in the alleged enterprise, but rather that it was entrusted to belligerent officers generally, and that prisoner was one of those officers, but not that he was personally directed to undertake or engage in the enterprise. And he added that the expedition may have put forward as a pretence, under the cloak of which to commit robbery. "The instructions to the officers to undertake the expedition were to abstain from violating any of the laws of this country in relation to neutrality; that the prisoner, and those engaged with him, did not act on those instructions, but in disregard to our laws, under the pretence of being peaceable citizens, embarked on board a vessel of a, to us, neutral friendly Power, with concealed arms, and by force captured the vessel, and in violation of the laws of war took from the prosecutor, a private individual and a non-combatant, a considerable sum of money. That this act of robbery was not at all necessary for them in carrying out the alleged enterprise, if they really had intended to carry it out, and therefore, taking the justification set up by the prisoner himself, on the ground put by his counsel, it failed". Adding that, "looking at all the facts as they are presented on either side, the conduct of those parties, and what they said and did during that time the vessel was in their possession, {and the insignificant number of persons},... in the most favourable view suggested for the prisoner, be a matter for the consideration of a jury whether they were acting in good faith in carrying out a belligerent enterprise, or whether they were not cloaking an expedition for the purposes of plunder under pretence of a belligerent enterprise, thinking in that way more readily to escape detention... and though the Confederate States are not recognised as independent, they are recognised as a belligerent power, and there can be no doubt that parties really acting on their behalf would be justified. But the case is one of piracy by the law of nations, in which case the men cannot be given up, because they can be tried here, or it is a case of an act of warfare, in which case they cannot be tried at all ...We must assume that parties will have a fair trial after their surrender, or we ought not to deliver them up at all, or to have agreed to do so".

Mr Justice Hagarty judged: "The evidence against the prisoner shows that a violent act of trespass has been committed on person and property, and a man has been robbed within the United States jurisdiction, and the person charged with these acts is found here. The learned Recorder has found that the evidence sufficient to warrant his being arrested and committed to abide the action of the executive under the Treaty. We are asked now to say that there is no evidence legally warranting such action. On the merits the defence is that the alleged robbery was simply an exercise of a belligerent right in taking money from a prisoner of war – that it was a mere subordinate incident in a lawful act of hostility, viz., the capture of any enemy's vessel on an expedition for the further capture of a war-ship and the release of Confederate prisoners". In considering this plea "I will assume that the documents from Richmond given in evidence are genuine. It becomes most important to consider whether the prisoner when he took Ashley's money was in good faith proceeding on the warlike enterprise in question, or was he using it as a pretext to cover vulgar robbery… The alleged assumption of responsibility for his act by his superiors, is rather a matter between them and the United States, than between the latter and us. It might be a dangerous course for a neutral to accept as conclusive, from a belligerent power with whom it has no diplomatic relations, an avowal of acts so very equivocal as those of the prisoner, and so opposed to the ordinary ideas of modern warfare… Had this prisoner been arrested on the wharf in Detroit, as he stepped onto the "Philo Parsons," and avowed and proved his character of a Confederate officer, he would have been in imminent danger of the martial rule applicable to a disguised enemy…if {they had been} captured in the act, {they would} have great difficulty in maintaining their right to be treated as prisoners of war, with no further responsibility".

Mr Justice John Wilson concluded that "The prisoner is charged with robbery, which is "The felonious taking of money or goods of any value from the person of another against his will, by violence, or putting him in fear of purpose to steal the same". That he is guilty prima facie has not been denied; and being here, his counsel says he is a British subject, and cannot be sent beyond the kingdom for trial, and the Treaty is not broad enough to cover his case. Secondly, he says he is a belligerent, and claims his rights as such; first, because he holds a warrant as Acting Master in the Navy of the Confederate States of America; second, the seizure of the steam vessel the "Philo Parsons" was an act of war undertaken with intent to liberate certain Confederate prisoners of war, confined on Johnson's Island, near Sandusky, on Lake

Erie; third, that the act of robbery charged is at most an excess, and at all events merged in the higher belligerent act; fourth, he says that although he can show no order directing what he did, he has a manifesto signed by the President of Confederate States, assuming the act by these States, and therefore he is not subject to committal for extradition under the Treaty … and lastly he says the warrant of commitment contains no adjudication that the evidence sustains the charge". He adds that, "The learned Recorder had equal jurisdiction with the judges of the superior courts of law to commit the prisoner for surrender under the Treaty, … it is proper that a matter of public interest should be settled so as to remove doubt." With regard to the prisoner "being a British subject, … assassins, incendiaries, and robbers are seized everywhere at the desire of the Sovereign in whose territories the crime was committed, and are delivered up to his justice. But the words of the Treaty are "all persons" who shall be charged with any of the crimes mentioned in the Treaty shall be surrendered. There can be no doubt but that the words of the Treaty include British subjects, for it was made in accordance with the law of nations."

"The prisoner {claims he} held a commission as Acting Master in the navy of the Confederate States. The holding of this or any other commission does not authorise him…, to wage warfare from a neutral territory on the unoffending and non-belligerent subjects of the country at war with the nation whose commission he holds. The evidence fails to prove such a commission. {With regard to the evidence,} What is there in all this which constitutes the act of war? If the object were to release the prisoners, from all that appears they never were nearer than 14 miles to Johnson's Island. Was the seizure of this unarmed boat per se an act of war? - for it has been argued that the robbery was merged in the higher act. The seizure of the boat, for whatever purpose, was one thing; the robbery of Ashley quite another; and in no way that we see, in furtherance of the design now insisted upon, necessary for its accomplishment. But is not the bona fide of the enterprise a matter of defence which a jury ought not to try? Such a trial can only be had where the offence was committed, and we cannot doubt but that justice will be fairly administered."

Consequently, as a result of the above arguments the judges granted extradition, but the decision was not popular in Canada and resulted in public demonstrations.

After the Judges discussions, the following letter was published in the Toronto Leader as a statement of the case;-

To the Editor of "The Leader".
"Sir, in the case of Burley the courts have decided in favour of his extradition on the charge of robbery. This decision is sustained exclusively by the testimony of Ashley, clerk of the steamer "Philo Parsons", Burley only urging as a defence the admitted fact that, at the time of the alleged robbery, he was acting under the orders of the Confederate States, whose officer he was, on an expedition for the release of his fellow soldiers, prisoners of war at Johnson's Island. As this expedition was for the glorious and noble purpose of releasing them from a captivity, the suffering and cruelty of which is so notorious as to have attracted the attention and enlisted the sympathy of the people of England, and as the expedition was in no sense for plunder, and there really was none, I beg to call public notice to the following statement of a gentleman engaged in the expedition as to what did actually occur, in order that the public may be possessed of the truth in the case. The gentleman making this statement is a man of the highest honour and truth; and though he was not produced on the trial as a witness, for obvious reasons, yet his recitals, independent of the intrinsic truth they bear on their face, can be fully substantiated. He says:-
"Immediately after leaving Kelly's Island the "Philo Parsons" was taken possession of in the name of the Confederate States. There was no violence used, and passengers were publicly informed that themselves and their property would be perfectly safe. The ladies and gentlemen accompanying them were permitted to remain under guard in the ladies cabin, and were told that they would be put ashore at the first convenient landing. While boarding at Middle Bass Island the steamer "Island Queen" came alongside, and lashed herself to the "Parsons". It being a matter of necessity, we took possession of her, capturing some 30 Federal soldiers. After wooding, the passengers were all put ashore, the soldiers having been paroled not to bear arms against the Confederate States until exchanged. Before setting the passengers ashore I asked them if any of them had been despoiled of any property, and they all replied that nothing had been taken from any of them. We then left Middle Bass Island, the "Island Queen" in tow of the "Parsons". We afterwards scuttled the "Queen", and turned her adrift. We then steered for Sandusky Bay, for the purpose of capturing the United States war steamer "Michigan", then lying off Johnson Island, guarding the prisoners confined there. A messenger was to have met us at Kelly's

Island, but failed to do so, for the reason that the officer in charge of the movement at Sandusky had been discovered and arrested that afternoon on board the "Michigan". In addition we were to have received signals from Sandusky Bay. Failing to receive the signals, a consultation was held; and it being feared that the plan had been betrayed, and the "Michigan" could not be surprised, it was determined to abandon the attack. We were at that time in full view of the "Michigan". The "Parsons" was then put about and steered for the Detroit River. The intention was to burn the boat, but the risk of injury to British vessels and property induced us to desist, and we ran her to Sandwich, where she was abandoned. One of the passengers captured, giving his name has C.K. Minor, of Jully, New York, had a large amount of money, represented to me as $80,000, on his person. He expressed considerable uneasiness, and was intimating a proposition whereby he could save a part, but I told him the object of the expedition was not robbery or plunder, but the release of prisoners on Johnson's Island, and not one cent was taken from him. Another man, name not remembered, who was a sheriff or revenue officer, had exhibited on the passage a large role of money, probably as much as $30,000. Not one cent of it was taken. Mrs Favan, wife of Hon J.J. Favan, Editor of the Cincinnati "Enquirer", was on board, and expressed to me her gratification at the polite and gentlemanly conduct of all the men engaged in the expedition. I positively deny the statement of Mr Ashley, clerk of the "Philo Parsons"; it is false that Mr Burley was in the office with Captain Beall, and false that Burley took $20, or any sum from him. Burley was at the time stationed at another part of the boat. What did occur was that Captain Beall and myself told Ashley that, having captured the boat, we considered the property of the boat as lawful prize, and we demanded from him the boats money. He handed over to us something about $90, reserving as much more, which he said was his individual property, and which he was permitted to keep. The whole amount taken was but a few dollars in excess of what we had paid him in the morning for our passage. Burley was dressed in dark coloured clothing, while I was dressed in light-coloured clothes. Burley had no whiskers.

Burley in his application to the Recorder for time to send to Richmond, makes oath that he took no money from Ashley, and it is most clear that he is innocent of this charge. Ashley swears that Burley was dressed in light-coloured clothing, and had whiskers, while Nichols, the mate of the "Parsons", and he is the only other witness to testify as to what occurred on the boat, swears that Burley was dressed in dark coloured clothing and had no whiskers. It is charity to Ashley to say that he is mistaken as to the man who took the money. Is it reasonable, or rather it is not manifestly absurd, that this expedition should be characterised as one intended for robbery, or for any other than a legitimate military enterprise, when persons in the power of this company, known to be in possession of thousands and tens of thousands of dollars are permitted to go off with their money, and Burley and his associates should content themselves with the stealing of the paltry $20 greenback? In the eyes of any fair-minded man, does this transaction wear any of the badges of robbery, for which one is to be now denounced as infamous. Burley is not charged with robbery in the United States, but the proceedings against him there are for piracy, as is shown by the testimony of Mr Alfred Russell, United States Attorney, and if he is given up, he will be tried for that offence, the penalty of which is death. In Canada he was first arrested upon a warrant sworn to charging him with attempting to murder the engineer of the "Island Queen". That was abandoned; he was then arrested upon sworn information charging him with robbery of clothing from Nichols, the mate, but when Nichols came he would not swear as had been sworn for him, and that charge was abandoned, and he was then arrested upon the charge of robbing Ashley, as false as the others. It must be apparent that the charges in Canada were mere pretext to secure the extradition to the United States where he is to be tried up on a charge that will take away his life, and when the brave Scotchman who has volunteered to fight the battles of the oppressed and downtrodden as well in the old country as in this, is delivered all to the relentless and cruel vindictiveness of the enemy seeking his life for an act born in the line of his duty, will not Canadians feel that their hands are stained with his blood. No attempt is made in this communication to attack the judgement of the courts, or to impeach their honesty, but it is simply to show how in the discharge of what they conceive to be their duty, a true innocent man's life is forfeited; and I verily believe that day will come when these judges and the people will feel and know that they have committed a grave error in delivering up this noble and gallant young Briton to the sacrifice".

(Signed), "JUSTICE".

Part D - The American trial

On February 2nd 1865, Burley was taken from Toronto to the Detroit House of Correction, where he stayed for six months, whilst the American authorities decided what to do with him. Burley is described at this time as being about 28, with a smooth, frank and open, almost girlish face. He was of medium height and robust appearance, "wearing a peculiar smile of daredevil, spoil-for-a-fight cussedness upon his countenance." While in confinement at Detroit he was said to have studied the French and German languages.

During Burleys incarceration in Detroit, his father sought British intervention. In a letter forwarded to the Foreign Office on February 24, 1865, he confirmed his fears, asking the Government to ensure that his son, given up on a charge of theft, would be charged with theft, and not piracy which would have been punishable by death. The letters of correspondence between Robert Burley and the various Government departments, including those of Canada and the USA, were presented to the House of Commons by command of Her Majesty on July 5th, 1876. The letters went all the way to the top, Earl Russell (the then prime minister for two terms) was heavily involved. The Governments stance was that "Her Majesty's Government will so far exert their good offices on his son's behalf as to endeavour to secure that he shall not be tried on any other charge than that on which the claim was made for his extradition"… the "Government are of the opinion that if the United States Government, having obtained the extradition of Burley on the charge of robbery, do not put him on his trial upon this charge, but upon another, viz., piracy (which if it had been made before the Canadian authorities they might have held not sufficiently established to warrant his extradition), this would be a breach of good faith against which Her Majesty's Government might justly remonstrate. If, however, the United States Government does bona fide put Burley on his trial for the offence in respect of which he was given up, it seems to Her Majesty's Government that it would be difficult to question the right of the Government to put him upon his trial for piracy also, or any other offence which he may be accused of having committed within their territory, whether such an offence was or was not a ground for extradition, or even within the Treaty." - It was also noted, that under another international treaty, the USS Michigan was only supposed to have one gun and not 15, as noted by the Canadians.

BENNET BURLEY PICTURED AT HIS TRIAL

On the 24th March, Robert Burley wrote directly to the Prime Minister from his home in Glasgow. Mr Burley was naturally anxious as he believed that his son could be sentenced to death after being surrendered on a minor offence on the evidence of one man. He went on to claim of his son, that he was "certain that he is innocent of this charge", and that "Ashley's evidence was loose and often contradictory, and on important points directly opposed to that of Nicholls, the mate of the steamer," and that "none saw the robbery, but Ashley and those who took the money; the charge rests solely on his testimony, and could have been disproven had witnesses been free to give evidence in Canada."

On March 20, 1865, a Mr Seward, of the Department of State, Washington replied to the British Government, stating that "… The Honourable the Attorney-General informs me that it is his purpose to bring the offender to trial in the Courts of the State of Ohio and Michigan for the crimes committed by him against the municipal laws of those states, namely, robbery and assault, with intent to commit murder. He was delivered up by the Canadian authorities upon a requisition which was based on charges of those crimes, and also upon a charge of piracy, which is triable not by State Courts, but by the Courts of the United States. I am not prepared to admit the principal claimed in the protest of Her Majesty's Government, that the offender could not legally be tried for the crime of piracy under the circumstances of the case. Nevertheless, the question raised upon it has become an abstraction, as it is at present the purpose of the Government to bring him to trial for the crimes against municipal law only". The British Government then argued "that in the warrant issued by the Governor of Canada, there is no appearance of any assault with intent to commit murder. There is a charge that Burley assaulted Ashley, and "put him in bodily fear and danger of his life", and there is a charge of robbery". The Canadian Government later confirmed to the British that the warrant for extradition was for robbery only.

Burley senior again wrote to the Prime Minister, this time he was concerned that the trial had been postponed several times and was now dated to take place on June 6th, bringing Bennet's total imprisonment to 7 or 8 months in Canada and the United States; he felt this unjust as "even the official correspondence (both British and American) clearly shows the act to have been a belligerent act. All other cases of similar character have been treated by British authorities as such; in fact, his is the solitary case, so far I have yet learned, of a belligerent being surrendered by a neutral Power." At this point, Burley senior referred the British Government to a similar case that occurred a month after the Philo Parsons affair that occurred in St Albans, Vermont, 15 miles south of the Canadian border.

It was here that 21 Confederate agents in civilian clothes entered the town which was had been largely untouched by the civil war. On October 19th three banks were robbed of about $200,000. The men tried to burn the village using four-ounce bottles of "Greek Fire", but when they smashed their bottles against the buildings, the mix would not burn, and they only managed to set fire to a woodshed. The men then re-entered Canada on horses stolen from the villagers, killing one villager and injuring another. The Canadian authorities tracked down and arrested 14 of the raiders, but did not turn them over to U.S. authorities, declaring that the raiders were soldiers under military orders, and let them go. Their goal was to gather cash for the Confederate treasury and to divert federal troops away from the Confederate armies in order to protect the northern border. The Canadian Government did return $88,000 to the banks that was found on the raiders.

On June 2nd 1865, Burleys father again wrote to the British Prime Minister, this time he enclosed a copy of a letter written by Burley to a friend in Canada from the Detroit House of Correction on 30th April, 1865, in which he wrote, "Last Thursday afternoon my irons were removed from my feet, and permission granted me to promenade along the gallery on which my cell is. Since then they have been very kind, permitting me to take a few hours exercise every day in the same way. Already I am feeling considerably bettered by this privilege in many ways. You can have no idea how much I enjoy my daily walk, it makes me almost dream. I have acquired new renewed life and hope. I have just returned from service in the prison chapel. I assure you it seemed like old times going to church once more, and hearing the dear Sabbath bells ringing the same glad welcome as of old…I can now understand, as I previously surmised, the spirit that prompted that offer of pardon, through such a worthy messenger as proposed it; though, of course, I cannot but feel delighted at being made the recipient of such intended kindness, and flattered at the projected honour that was to have been done me…How often may we, with equal truth, exclaim with the sage, "God preserve us from our friends!"

A letter on June 10th set out that Burley had been indicted in the County of Ottawa, of Ohio, for robbery, and was also indicted in the United States District Court for Eastern District of Michigan for robbery on the high seas and for piracy. However, the United States District Attorney thought the indictments flawed and that he would never be tried on them; "for the reasons that these offences are not predictable upon any acts committed on inland waters." The British had a slight technical problem, British Admiralty Law defined piracy as occurring on the "high seas", which meant salt water, there was therefore no provision for piracy on a fresh water lake.

However, by now, larger world events had come in to play; at

Appomattox on April 9th 1865, General Lee surrendered and the Civil War was now over; the men Burley had sought to liberate from the island were on their way back home. It now seemed that The US Government had become disposed to extend leniency towards Burley, and had it not been for the recent assassination of President Lincoln, he would possibly have been acquitted before the Ohio Tribunal.

On July 10th Burley was brought once again to Sandusky Bay and then transferred to Port Clinton where quite a large crowd had gathered to see the man who had caused such an international diplomatic row. He was accompanied by his counsel, Sylvester Larned and Rufus P. Ranney. Port Clinton is the county seat of Ottawa County, Ohio, whose boundaries included the Bass Islands, so the robbery in question must have been seen to be accomplished while the Philos Parsons was at or near Middle Bass Island. A week later the trial commenced with the grand jury at Port Clinton, Ohio, indicting Burley on three counts, including robbery and assault.

The opening arguments of the trial included statements that a state of war existed; that the Confederate States were in existence long before the alleged act by the conspirators had been committed; that Burley was appointed an Acting Master in the Confederate Navy, and was serving in that capacity, under the direction of his superior, Captain J. Y. Beall; that the purpose of the exploit was to capture the USS Michigan and release the prisoners on Johnson's Island, in an expedition authorised by the Confederate government; that Burley was liable to the Federal government only as a prisoner of war, or to a military tribunal. Also it was stated that an indictment for the same offence was pending in Detroit; and that the court there had assumed jurisdiction, and that he was removed to Port Clinton against his will.

Clerk Walter Ashley was one of the witnesses, and he told the story of the fateful trip of the Philos Parsons from Detroit on Monday, September 19, 1864; Captain Orr of the Island Queen told the story of his boats capture at Middle Bass, and the treatment of the captives. Another witness, William Rehburg of Middle Bass Island, was a passenger from his island to Sandusky. He told how Burley pointed a pistol at him and ordered him below, and told him of the conspirators objective. The commission of Burley as an Acting Master was presented; so was the document acknowledging the official character of the raid as an expedition of the Confederate government, signed by President Davis.

The telling points of the defence counsels arguments were that the men came on board with arms and grappling irons; why would the men want grappling irons in order to commit a private robbery? - Captures on the high seas included all money belonging to the boat, and no discrimination could be made between the private money of the clerk and that which belonged to the boat. If they had intended robbery on their own account, they would have robbed the rest of the passengers.

The Judge summarised the case by saying that "a state of war existed between the Federal Government and the Confederate Government so called, and it made no difference whether the United States Government admitted it or not, the rights of belligerents must be accorded them". The charge now made was only applicable to a state of war; was this man only executing the orders of his Government? If so, having conferred upon him the power, it would take away the right to punish him under civil law. "As a soldier of the Confederate States Government, he had a soldier's right to capture the steamer, and appropriate her, and any money belonging to her, to the cause of his Government..."

With regard to stealing for his own personal benefit, his commission as Acting Master would not protect him, "but the theft must be found to have been made with felonious intent; the intent was one thing, and the act another."

"Going on the boat in disguise would make no difference. Men must have authority for taking the lives of persons". The only act the jury had to look to was the robbery charge. He had a right, if commissioned, to take the boat, money or the property for the furtherance of his Government, but not for his own private purpose.

After deliberating for five hours, the jury reported that it could not agree, and was split six and six by one account and eight to four for his conviction in another. Burleigh was remanded to prison and bail fixed at $3000. No bail was furnished, and Burley remained in custody for some time, awaiting a second trial expected in the October.

On July 18th, the British Delegation in Washington sent the following extract from the New York "Daily News" of July 17, 1865, to the British Prime Minister; "The trial of Bennet G Burley, one of the Lake Erie raiders, for robbing while on board the steamer "Philo Parsons", in

September last, commenced at Port Clinton, Ohio, on Tuesday, and was concluded the following day. The trial resulted very satisfactorily - to Burley - and which will doubtless be the last we shall hear of that noted individual. The case was tried in the Court of Common Pleas, Judge Fitch, of Toledo, presiding; and the evidence in the case was substantially the same as has previously been published. The Judge charged the jury in substance as follows:- That if they found that Burley was a regularly commissioned officer in the Confederate States Navy, and that none of the property seized had been used for private purposes, they must bring in a verdict of not guilty. He charged also that Burley, if he was commissioned as aforesaid, had a perfect right to organise a hostile expedition on neutral territory...Notwithstanding this curious and surprising charge, eight of the jurors favoured a verdict of guilty. Four, however, kept on the opposite tack: and after a deliberation of half an hour, the jury returned to the Court, and announced that they could not agree on a verdict. The jury was discharged, the prisoner remanded into the custody of the authorities, and the second trial set down for the October term of the Court. The prisoner asked permission to give bail, and prosecuting attorney Annesley, required that he should enter into $500 bonds, with two sureties of his appearance for trial! (Very modest, prosecuting Attorney, that!) Mr Russell asked, or rather suggested, that the same bail which had been fixed in this State at $8000, should be required. The Judge, under the circumstances, compromised the matter, and fixed the bail at $3000."

The result of the trial wasn't popular with another newspaper, The Detroit Tribune editorialised: "The interesting question now is, who is "Judge" Fitch of Toledo? ... The decision... is a judicial outrage and disgrace. It is an open and positive justification of piracy, and is in all respects atrocious... Where was Judge Fitch when all these facts were transpiring? Was he insane, was he drunk; was he in the rebel army; was he making Copperhead speeches - where was he? Judge Fitch evidently needs looking after. If he is an ignoramus he ought to be removed. If he is a rebel sympathiser he ought to be impeached. We may be pardoned, in this locality, for some feeling upon the subject of this decision..." Incidentally, the Sandusky Register disagreed with the Detroit Tribune and thought the case was decided in line with the authorities, but observed that the offence really belonged in the United States court and not in the Ohio court.

On August 11th, Burleys father again wrote to the British Prime Minister. He was concerned that thanks to the disagreement of the jury his son was remanded to prison, for another trial (which was scheduled for October), unless bail to the amount of $3000 was furnished. He was also concerned at reports that he himself had been largely and successfully engaged in the blockade running, and that a deposit of money, to the amount asked, could be readily given by him. He argued that these reports were devoid of truth and that it was apparent that money as an equivalent for his release, is what was really wanted; an amount which was out of his power to give. He believed that it was "clear that a sum of money as bail to be forfeited, is what is wanted by those who hold him in custody, a sort of ransom in fact". Mr Burley continued to argue that his sons defence had already cost his relatives and friends considerable sums, and exhausted what they could do for him in that way. However, in the final letter from the British Government, dated September 22nd, the British Government stated that they could not interfere. So bail was neither furnished or forfeited. The rumours of Burley senior being involved in blockade running could have come from the fact the first confederate blockade running ship, the Fingal was purchased, sailed and filled with armaments from his childhood home town of Greenock, near Glasgow. Many other Confederate ships, such as the Shenandoah were also built in Glasgow.

In the meantime, Burleigh had become friends with the Port Clinton Sheriff who enjoyed Burleys company so much that he took him out with him to town; the people of the town also liked his company: and his mail was handed to him through a jail window, either to save the Sheriff the embarrassment of examining his letters or to make him unable to examine them. Locals also turned up with food and to have a chat through the cell windows. On one occasion the sheriffs wife whilst leaving the jail caught sight of two young women chatting to Burley through his cell window, and although they departed too quickly to be recognised one was identified later from a letter found in Burleys cell. Apparently he was also discovered with a table knife which he had fashioned into a saw. Burleighs cell was located at the centre of the first floor of the Port Clinton Courthouse, which was entered through a door at the end of a small hall leading from the courthouse; the Sheriff, and his family also lived off the small hall, in a series of the rooms on either side . On the outside of the entrance to the jail was a sheet-iron door, inside which was a door made of bar iron, running crosswise, about 6 inches apart. All in all, the building was quite a poor structure. On Sunday, September 17, 1865, the Sheriff and his family left for a short visit to the country, and he locked the inside door to the jail, pushing the sheet-iron door shut and placing the padlock in the staple without turning the key, and giving Burley, who was apparently the sole occupant, the freedom of the jail hall. About five o'clock the Sheriff sent a man to give Burley his supper, but the keys in the Sheriff's bedroom were missing - and so was Burley. The window east of the hall door on the south end of the jail was raised, propped up by a crotched stick cut from a nearby apple tree; showing that he had received outside help; the sheet-iron door and the bar iron door were both unlocked, but Burley had left this note on his Bible:

Sunday-I have gone out for a walk-
Perhaps (?) I will return shortly.

B.G. Burley

Burley had escaped after being held at Port Clinton for a total of about 3 months, the escape being just two days short of the first anniversary of the Lake Erie raid. The Sheriff spent about $100 to recapture Burley, and ultimately one William Mulcahy of Bay Township acknowledged that he had hidden and cared for Burley for a week or two (though this was apparently common knowledge amongst the townsfolk who didn't like the idea of more of the local taxpayers money being spent on another trial), and finally took him disguised to Detroit and across the river to Windsor, he was expecting to be well rewarded for his services, but never heard from Burley again. Burley soon returned to Scotland, and as the war had ended, many people seemed glad he had escaped, including the County Commissioners, who despaired of Burley's conviction and were tired of paying for his maintenance. Some time later, the Sheriff received a letter from Burley in Canada asking him to send the books which he had left in his cell, and in order to try and get some of his money back, the Sheriff responded that if Burley would send him some money, he would forward the books. The money came (thanks to his exploits Burleigh had been paid a large sum of money by the Southern Congress) and the sheriff sent the books, thus closing the incident; though as a matter of fact, there was no legal conclusion to the case, which as a result is still open.

A local Justice, Justice Brown said that Burley had sent other residents in the neighbourhood tokens of his appreciation. Some 40 years later, in the midst of the Russian Japanese war, Justice Brown, now of the United States Supreme Court, said he was following the events in Manchuria for some "wild adventure" of Bennet Burleigh.

This was not the end of the story, Burleys co-conspirator Beall, was less fortunate. Beall was captured whilst trying to derail a train near Buffalo. On February 10, 1865, a court martial convened to try Beall on two charges: violating the law of war by capturing a civilian ship and acting as a spy. He insisted that he had honourably worked under the orders of President Jefferson Davis and authorized agents of the Confederate Government. The court ignored his defence, found him guilty, and sentenced him to death. Despite great pressure, President Lincoln failed to mitigate, suspend or delay Bealls sentence. The Virginia historical Society has claimed that Beall and John Wilkes Booth, the actor, were friends (upon his arrested Booth was found with a bill of exchange from a Montreal bank, dated October 27th 1864) and that Booth had pleaded with President Lincoln to spare Bealls life. The Federal Secretary of State said that public sentiment demanded Bealls execution, and that he would resign if the President interfered; so Beall was hanged, and the terrible effect on Booth led to him brooding vengeance and his assassination of President Lincoln. His diary however is said to contain an item, which in itself controverts this story; Booth is said to have written: "I knew no private wrong, I struck for my country and that alone."

In 1868, back home in Glasgow, Burley, changed his name to Burleigh, which he held to be the proper spelling, and again met his old friend, now General McIver, with whom he had aided Garibaldi's invasion of Naples, this soldier of fortune was, by the end of his life, to have served under no fewer than 18 different flags. At this time, a Cretan insurrection was going on, and Burleigh mentioned that he was thinking of getting up an expedition to help them. It was agreed that MacIver should proceed to Crete, in order to obtain a commission to organise a body of troops for service. The Cretans were only too glad to accept the assistance and he received a commission from the provisional government: "… we give for power to Colonel Henry Ronald MacIver to make war on land and sea against the enemies of Crete, and particularly against the Sultan of Turkey, and the Turkish forces, and to burn, destroy, or capture any vessel bearing the Turkish flag, and permission to choose and command his officers and men". Upon his return to Glasgow, MacIver found Burleigh and a large number of others ready to join him, but unfortunately, the Turkish ambassador got wind of the affair and prevented them from getting the ship they required to carry out the expedition. Having no chance in Britain, MacIver returned to the Mediterranean with two or three Scotsman, determined to try and organise a daring team of raiders at Piraeus, near Athens, the purpose being to seize a Turkish gunboat. However, when they reached Athens, they found out that the Turkish government had quelled the Cretan insurrection, and that other volunteers were already returning home. Burleigh's plans to help liberate Crete, were therefore cancelled.

When Burleigh eventually returned from America, a family story goes, that he asked his father if he was still "bothered with wood", and upon the affirmative, he presented him with some American hickory, which, due to it being very hard, stiff, dense and shock resistant, brought about a revolution in the handle and walking stick industry. Burley was the first to appreciate the properties of hickory, and the material was seen as so suitable for handle making, that Burley arranged for his son to purchase large quantities in the States and ship it home. The handles were marketed under the trade mark Texana, and sold in huge numbers. A company was set up with a capital of £15,000, which was made up of units of £10 shares, and after his "visit home", Burleigh was sent back to America to use this money to set up a mill in Rock Creek, Ohio where hickory logs were cut into planks before shipping; The company then opened a larger mill being later built in Dermott, Arkansas and another in Dawson, Kentucky; (these mills were not disposed of by the family until 1919, one being sold to Burleighs son Sherer who continued to supply the family business back in Scotland). Business done, Burleigh then made his way to Texas where he undertook his first real journalistic work as one of the editors of the Houston Telegraph, the last great bastion of Confederate News. During this time, he also aligned himself with the British Government trying to interest Englishmen to emigrate to Texas. It appears that Burleighs past indiscretions in the United States had now been forgotten, or perhaps he was covered by his name change. As a friend of his concluded, "It has never be possible to get a clear and consistent story of the young fire-eaters adventures during those stirring times {in America}. He seems, from his own accounts, for the most part to have been a perpetual prisoner of war in a chronic state of being under sentence of death. In spite of this vicious treatment he lived to squander his military yearnings in many other fields and to reach a ripe old age." It seems that Burleigh, like most of his companions who were in the habit of facing dangers, rarely spoke of themselves even to intimate friends, and Burleigh never spoke publicly of his adventures around lake Erie. Though he did comment on the matter, at his retirement dinner, with the quiet humour which contributed so largely to his popularity, remarking that "the sentences and myself, were never executed."

During his stay in Texas, the Franco German War broke out and Burleigh left America once again for Europe in order to serve with France in the Franco German War. He received a commission but only joined the 'Army of the Loire' just before the armistice was arranged. He once again returned to America, and for some years in the 1870's, he worked for the New York Sun, famous for the line on journalistic endeavour penned by its editor, "When a dog bites a man, that is not news, because it happens so often. But if a man bites a dog, that is news."

Once he had earned his journalistic spurs, Burleigh once again returned to the British Isles, and the love of war and dangerous adventure combined with his physical attributes, and remarkable ability to pick up languages and dialects pointed the way for him to start leading what would be a remarkable life and career as a war correspondent. Less than 4 years after returning to England, he found himself in standing in the sands of North Africa.

Chapter 3 - The Sudan
Part A - First steps in Africa

"What a land the Sudan is! As a sorely tired friend said to me, after passing a succession of sleepless nights owing to the dust and rain storms, and overburdened days because of the heat, " What do the British want in this country? Is it the intention of the Government to do away with capital punishment and send all felons here? I am not surprised the camel has the hump." - Bennet Burleigh (1898)

Burleigh was to become a war correspondent in the age of the telegraph which changed and aided journalistic style. The correspondent Archibald Forbes said of this new style of journalism that, "However interesting a battle may be, you must always get away before your communications are cut, for your material will be held up or never arrive. You must not be taken prisoner, for then you will be out of business completely. You must not get wounded, for then you will be a useless expense to your paper. And if you get killed, you will be an infernal fool." and as Burleigh himself was to put it, "it is an age of hurry, and the war correspondents are in the running."

During his career Burleigh wrote several books on about some of the major wars he attended, all of which were widely read by the public. In the introduction of his first book, "Desert Warfare" chronicling the record of the battles of the Eastern Sudan campaign of February and March 1884, Burleigh gives a brief insight into his earlier trips to Egypt and the Sudan, and also outlines his reasoning and journalistic style. He claims he first visited Egypt in July 1882, as a war correspondent in order to chronicle the incidents in the campaign that terminated in the victory at Tel el Kebir. This first visit likely coincided with the bombardment and invasion of Alexandria by the British. On May 20th, an Anglo-French fleet arrived at Alexandria causing a heightening of tension and a deadly riot in the city. The British commanders blamed Arabi Pasha, (a soldier who had gained control of the government, as a wave of anti foreign sentiment swept across the country), and his supporters. On July 11th the British fleet commenced their bombardments and on July 13, a large naval force landed in the city and despite heavy resistance the British eventually forced the Egyptians to withdraw.

Burleigh visited this land twice more before he joined the little army commanded by General Graham which was occupied with the release of the beleaguered garrison at Tokar. During his second trip, Burleigh was present at the battle of Kassassin (September 10th 1882), and though he reached the wire first, the story goes that he did not have his release ready, so held up the line by requesting that the telegraph operator send the first chapter of Genesis until the real message was ready.

A few days later came the march to and surprise attack at Tel el Kebir which culminated in the end of power for Arabi Pasha, Burleigh gave London the first news of the events. "The night of September 12 was moonless, and the desert was wrapped in a grey gloom which the eye could not pierce. Due west from the camp of Sir Garnet Wolseley a line of engineered telegraph posts had been erected for half a mile or more. As the advance, or guiding column, moved away from the camp, these posts would start them in the right direction. At the end they would swing clear and march by the stars. The total distance to Arabi's entrenchments was 6 miles. At 1.30 in the morning the column started and moved forward less than an hour, as a sort of experimental march. The plan worked marvellously well. The stars were brilliant. A naval officer steered the army in close formation with accuracy: there was no confusion. After a brief rest the march was resumed. The night now was very dark and the stars, which had been used for guidance a few hours before, were below the horizon. But the pole star was always visible and furnished a fixed point on the celestial chart. For an hour absolute silence reigned. During that final hour the tension became very severe; guiding stars dropped below the horizon one by one and others higher in the heavens had to be selected. These at times were covered by clouds, but the pole star over the right shoulder and the star in front for which the column was aimed, were never blotted from sight at the same time.

What might have easily been an awful catastrophe was averted by the good discipline of the force. An order for a few minutes halt was issued. At once the centre companies stopped, but the order required a little time to reach the outermost companies on the flanks, and they continued to advance, always keeping in touch with the man next in toward the centre. When all were halted, therefore, the force lay on the desert almost in a half circle, and as the word to start was given again the companies on the flanks moved forward and found themselves face-to-face. In the dim light a single false move might have pre-precipitated terrible consequences. At precisely the instant desired the camp of the unsuspecting Egyptians was reached. A single shot broke the dead silence. Five minutes after the firing of that shot, the dawn had begun and after five more minutes the entire landscape was revealed, for the desert dawn is very short".

The instant the battle was over Burleigh surveyed the trenches, and acquired a comprehensive notion of the disposition of the troops and the nature of the ground on which they had fought. Without losing a minute he began a hard ride to Kassassin across the deserts, where he knew he could command a telegraph wire. Over this he sent the first news of the battle. The message off, he remounted and made all haste back to the battleground, where he learned that the cavalry brigade had been ordered to Cairo. He rode on alone with such speed that he reached the city even before the advance guard, finding Arabi a prisoner and the war at an end. He hurried to the wire, but it was impossible to send the despatch by the native operators as they knew no English, so he borrowed a horse and started again for Kassassin. He rode through the night, Egyptian soldiers occasionally firing upon him, and Arabian robbers once or twice attempting his capture, and with 10 miles of desert between him and the wire his horse broke down; he walked the rest on foot, and wrote and sent away another important despatch. Over two sleepless days he had ridden 140 miles through hostile and desert country. It was an amazing exploit and it scored the greatest scoop of the time. His untiring energy and realistic descriptions established him in the public taste, thus establishing his reputation. Bennet Burleigh had "broken into the game" with a vengeance. He finished this trip riding with the cavalry into Cairo. The Egyptian army was beaten and shortly after the war Sir Evelyn Wood, became the Sirdar or Commander in Chief of these native Forces.

By now, Burleigh had now given two years service to the Central News Agency, he was their first correspondent and one of their directors; he had been involved in the crisis over Gladstone's Irish Home Rule Bill. In May 1882, he broke the news to the celebrating Irish delegation in Westminster, that on the eve of the Home Rule, a crisis was at hand; an

English Lord and Under Secretary had been murdered in Dublin's Phoenix Park, which had thus sent the process of Home Rule into free-fall. The delegation accused Burleigh of manufacturing a "bogus outrage for tomorrows Sunday Papers", but their worst fears were confirmed by someone else at 5am the following morning.

Immediately after the 1882 campaign, Burleigh left the Central News Agency; based on the strength of his experience in the American Civil War he had been invited to join the Daily Telegraph, the 1873 "discoverers" of the Loch Ness monster, and the most popular newspaper in the land at the time; Burleigh was to work for them through every war until his retirement; Lord Burnham, the owner of the Daily Telegraph regarded him as a very promising talent, and the strongest man he ever knew.

Burleigh continues to present his book, "Desert Warfare" as a collection of the largely unedited telegrams and letters in the form in which they were cabled and appeared in the Daily Telegraph, describing his forth visit and the happenings around the battles of El Teb, Tokar and Tamaai. In the books introduction he describes his style of writing, "that whether on foot or horseback my note-book and pencil were seldom out of my hand, if any movement was taking place … (it) was there and then inscribed", believing that the soldiers and the public valued the accuracy of his heat of the moment comments. In a later book he claims to have taken notes on a daily basis, sometimes hour by hour. He liked to think his work described campaign life well; "Such was the record made by me at the time … our round of life, its little excitements, and the situation of affairs as it at the time appeared to us in the wilds."

In Cairo in 1883, Burleigh was presented with his first reports regarding the rising of the Mahdi - the last of the prophets as foretold by Mohamed. In a town just south of Berber, Mahomet Achmed, (who was to become the Mahdi) an apprentice to his uncle, a boatman on the Nile, left for Khartoum after a beating. Here he joined a Medressu where he remained for some time studying his religion. After several years attending different schools, he had gained a reputation for sanctity, and was ordained a faki or sheikh in the 1870's. From here he began making a subterranean excavation (khaliva - retreat), where he would fast and pray. His fame spread far and wide and he collected many disciples and wives.

By about the end of May 1881, he wrote to other religious chiefs, claiming that he was the Mahdi, and that it was his divine mission amongst other things to reform Islam and convert the world to Islamism. He added that all who did not believe him should be destroyed, and urged the leaders to bring their men and join him. He began to alarm the authorities. Osman Digna became the Mahdi's lieutenant in Eastern Sudan; Osman was a fairly unremarkable trader until he had a run in with authorities and tried to incite some other slave dealers in Suakim to rebel. In 1883 whilst buying some native articles in the interior, he met the Mahdi and pledged allegiance, acknowledging him as the messiah. Osman soon attracted followers, and set up headquarters south of Suakim threatening local garrisons.

The British cabinet decided in early January, 1884, after a number of disastrous military defeats, that they should abandon all that lay south of the line drawn across Wadi Halfa in Northern Sudan; which is still approximately where the modern day Egypt – Sudan border lies. Sudan is a huge country, being around the same size as western Europe. This left some 20,000 Egyptian soldiers and 40,000 civilians at the mercy of the Mahdi's barbarians. At the beginning of February, the British army fighting under General Baker had been surprised and slaughtered by the Arabs at El Teb some 5 miles from Trinkitat; It was feared that the Mahdi's men, bold, confident and much better armed after these successive victories would soon attack upper Egypt via Suakim on the East African coast.

On February 15th, 1884, Burleigh set out for the Sudan. The journey being not so simple a job as it is today, he travelled by train, with mainly British officers headed for Cairo, through France and Switzerland and arriving 2 days later in Brindisi, Italy, where one could catch the mail steamer. Whilst waiting for the P&O mail steamer to depart, forward arrangements were made to Port Said at the head of the Suez canal, in order to meet a steamer to take them through the canal. The men arrived at Port Said three and a half days later after enduring quite a rough crossing, and boarded the steamer. By midnight they had reached Lake Timsah in the Suez canal. Here, the weather worsened, and Burleigh recalled that most of the passengers "still carry about the impressions made upon us that night" as they took shelter lying on their luggage in the little fore-cabin. In his memoirs, a fellow war correspondent, Frederick Villiers who travelled with Burleigh on this journey claims his associate was known for travelling light, taking with him little more than a toothbrush and some carbolic soap! They however pressed on into the canal proper, hoping they would still make the mail steamer for Suakim. The ship wasn't to leave for a few days, so they boarded another, The Northumbria. The rest of the trip was uneventful, bar having to sleep on deck, and hoping that they would catch up with the esteemed General Buller, who had won the Victoria Cross in the Zulu war.

As it turns out the correspondents got to Suakim ahead of Buller, who had had a three day head start on them, and they pushed on to Trinkitat, reaching this hostile place with no fresh water on February 26th. The British army were up to the water task though, using small tugs sat out in the bay they condensed the sea water. Burleigh came ashore and set to collecting his horses with the help of an old servant he had met at Suez, a Greek named Mekali; then he inspected the camp and made himself known to General Graham and his staff, who informed him that all correspondents were required to get a pass at the cost of a shilling to enable them to accompany the expedition. Burleigh spent the night back on the boat. Officially the British were going forward to relieve Tokar, but everyone knew that it had fallen, and the real task was to administer a drubbing to the Arabs, and to later capture Osman Digna at his base near Suakim. The following morning, Burleigh mounted up and went out alone in order to have a look at the outposts of Fort Baker some two miles away, where he received a cup of tea on arrival and information regarding the lay of the land to El Teb. He then rode forward to meet the scouts, and had his first welcoming from the enemy some 800 yards away, who took the odd pot shot at him.

The following day, Burleigh and his servant accompanied the troops out to Fort Baker carrying very little as they were to bivouac with the troops that night. He professes only to have carried a blanket, some biscuits, a tin of meat with a little something in his water bottle, a contradiction to some of the claims that he was teetotal. (He also mentions in his book Madagascar and Ashantee that he was a connoisseur of whisky; and the war artist Frederic Villiers also retells how Burleighs whisky saved him from the pain of a nasty scorpion bite on the road to Omdurman.) Burleigh spent the evening chatting with officers and seeing to the horses before finally bedding down on a pile of straw at 11pm, ready for the following days battle. The night was damp and the men were treated to an early morning tropical downpour. Reveille came at 5am, the fires were lit and breakfast was had in good spirits. At 8am the order was given to move forward for half a mile where the men formed a square with a front of about 350 yards. Burleigh rode forward with the scouts, the ground littered with the rotting corpses of Bakers soldiers who had tried to retreat just weeks before.

By 10.30am, some three miles from Fort Baker, the enemies earthworks were within 800 yards. The enemy opened the attack, but the British soldiers pressed on to their goal of passing the north face of the enemies works. At noon, the British bugles sounded the advance, and the enemy, mostly armed with spears and swords, fearless of death and full of fury rushed at the square, with only a few getting to within ten yards, as the front cleared, the British rushed into the fort where a fierce mêlée ensued. By one o'clock the British pushed forward to the fresh water mud holes at El Teb where the Mahdi's men made one last stand, falling to the British after three or four hours in total. The British had lost some 30 men, and the enemy about 1000. The British spent the night at El Teb, in order to reinforce before they pushed on to Tokar the following day. Burleigh had seen the days action from the square, and during the evening he followed the cavalry back to the fort in order to compare his notes with Headquarters staff, thus complying with the previous days general order that no reports of the fight could be wired to England that were not approved and signed by headquarters. Burleigh remarked that he hated this delay and worry, as he always wanted to get to the wire first; headquarters cut Burleighs casualty figures in half before they let him he ride off to Trinkitat with the first of the news. Here he spent several hours trying to get his messages out with little success, and eventually being forced to change his plans by passing his notes and a hefty tip to an Arab runner who reached Suakim by seven the next morning; here a senior naval officer gave the runner a receipt and sent a brief excerpt to London. One must bear in mind that the official despatches did not leave Trinkitat until six that morning, and all other messages were supposed to wait in line. Thus Burleigh gained prominence and his paper was able to give the news to the world in advance of all others.

That same morning, Burleigh headed back through El Teb and on towards Tokar. His horse was fresh, and the country appeared perfectly safe. He digresses at this point to describe his field kit, a dark blue suit, a water bottle, pockets full of biscuits, a toothbrush, carbolic soap, a towel, a pair of binoculars, and an army revolver with ammo; and then about his life in the field; after a nights bivouac a bath would be made from a hole in the sand and a waterproof sheet which would then be used by several men, with the left over water drunk by the horses. That morning at 9am the army moved out from El Teb reaching Tokar by 3pm, after trading a few shots, the Arabs ran out of the fort and headed towards Suakim, more than likely to join Osman Digna who had the town invested; the Arab deserters were closely followed by their grateful captives who thought they were going to be put to the slaughter until the British arrived.

Approaching Tokar, Burleigh and his associates ran into a group of mounted Arabs who had just vacated the fort, so they turned tail back to El Teb being chased for about an hour and though it came close, Burleigh and his party were never caught. The small party eventually reached the outskirts Tokar just as the British were in the process of taking it, being one of only two correspondents on the scene he couldn't believe his luck, as he would have all the news to himself.

That evening Burleigh returned to Tokar, and as night fell, the small party got worried about an ambush and not being able to find their destination, they pressed on however and eventually caught site of the British camp fires. Although the desert days were hot, the nights were cold and an uneasy sleep ensued, the men awoke due to the cold and huddled round a fire, nodding the hours away. As dawn broke the land warmed up, and a smart breakfast of cocoa, biscuits and corned meat was had. Burleigh and his fellow correspondent saddled up and headed out to the outlying villages, ransacking the abandoned native huts on the way. Burleigh procured himself a goody bag filled with both European and Arab curios, hats, horse trappings and musical instruments etc; a couple of goats were also procured in order to improve the evenings camp cuisine. His telegrams home described the foes way of living.

On the Sunday morning, after spies had reported spoils of war in several of the surrounding villages, a small squadron left the camp, amongst whom were Burleigh and General Buller. They discovered many native huts full of plunder including guns and ammunition. As the enemy seemed to have abundant provisions, several cattle, fowl and goats were procured for the camp. The British spent a few days in the area, resting, cleaning up, helping the injured and burying the dead. The boats at Trinkitat were ordered to coal up in order to be ready to set out to Suakim in a few days. Burleighs runner to Suakim had heard the natives bewailing their lost children and brothers, reproaching the Mahdi who had told them that bullets would not hurt them; it later turned out that Digna and the Mahdi said they had made a mistake as they had dealt out the wrong talismanic shirts and robes. It was however thought that a battle with Osman at Suakim would end the whole sad business.

The troops embarked for Suakim, it was hoped that given the defeat at El Teb, Osman Digna might come to terms if he witnessed a heavy troop presence there. Burleighs servant and two horses set off for Suakim again on the Northumbria, Burleigh followed later in the day (5th March) aboard the paddle steamer Sphinx. He was happy to get back from the wilds, and back to the edges of civilisation. Burleigh got ashore on the first gig going to shore and headed straight to the telegraph office to send a despatch. At which point the Admirals private secretary came in saying he had got into a row with the Admiral for letting him come ashore and get to the telegraph first before the official despatches were sent. Burleigh apologised for getting him into trouble and regretted the situation as the news that day was rather small and unimportant. Needless to say the message was stopped until the Admirals news was sent. This was a bit of a bugbear though for Burleigh, believing his news to be of just as much value. He then set off house hunting not wishing to spend the night in the dirty lanes of Suakim. Not long after starting his search a fellow correspondent approached him and asked if he wanted to share the lodgings with him in an Austrian ex-pat's house. It turns out that the Landlord, a Mr Levi, knew Osman Digna of old, and had recently visited his camp on behalf of the Egyptian Government. He said that Digna feared assassination, even from him, and was exceedingly devout. He asked Digna to stop the war and to discuss the situation with English officers, but he would not entertain the proposal. He was treated roughly by his "captors" but managed to give them the slip after about a week. Burleigh set up home on the third floor, using the roof terrace as a bath and dressing room, he even had the luxury of a bed and table. There were six Europeans in the house and being near to the causeway that linked Suakim to the mainland where the troops were stationed, they had a lot of visitors, and after a days news hunting, a dinner party and a "jolly sing-song" would be had. The antics in the house kept them all in good spirits. On a daily basis Burleigh would take his horses out around the camp, going a little further afield each day until one day his attention was called to two armed Arabs whom he circled and apprehend as prisoners, though it turns out the men were friendlies, which Burleigh found hard to bear.

Diplomatic moves to avert another battle came to nought, and so the enemy were not allowed long to recover from their defeat at El Teb. On around the 9th March, an advance zereba, made of low earthworks and mimosa was set up between Suakim and the enemies camp, and once the mule batteries could fill it with three days of supplies and water, the whole force would move to attack; but this proved not an easy task due to the intense heat.

On March 12th, the force set out for Osman Digna's stronghold in Tamaai. Burleigh travelled with his servant and two natives who carried white rags in hand in order to distinguish them from the enemy as they rode despatches back to Suakim. Later in the afternoon, Burleigh rode forward with the scouts, clearing the way for the infantry, though there were no enemy about. They rode up one of the low hills overlooking the valley of Tamaai, where, two miles away on the opposing low lying hills, they could plainly see their foe, estimated at some 5000 men, as opposed to the British having 4200. Back down in the foothills, the infantry were ordered to bivouac where they stood, and a new zereba made; along with plans to attack for the following morning. Come daybreak, the soldiers could see "hundreds of the black woolly heads of the savage foe, bobbing about among the bushes on the low ridges, scarcely 100 yards away." During the night, Burleigh was woken at 1am by the whizzing of hundreds of rifle bullets, it turned out only to be skirmish fire with few casualties, one unfortunate soldier was shot in the head as he lay down, but it was a shock to the system nonetheless and carried on until daybreak.

The following morning, at 8 am, the British advance from their bivouacs was quickly followed by a series of vicious fights, the enemies rush ensured confusion and British squares were checked causing the men to fall back up to 800 yards. Burleigh rode over to the corner of a failing square and remarked on how the enemy did their work; "Fearless and daring, they ran amuck, so to speak, at our men, hitting right and left even when themselves badly wounded. It was this very recklessness of death on their part which made them so dreaded". As the corner collapsed, Burleigh decided, "it was a time when ones country was of far greater importance than ones professional calling", so he did what he could for the former during the surging five minutes, shouting at the men in a language more forcible than choice, to try and rally them to close up and fire steadily. "I saw Arab after Arab, through whose bodies our bullets had ploughed their way, charging down on the square, with the blood spouting in pulsating streams from them at every heart-throb. Down they bore on us; some with two or three bullet wounds, reeling like frenzied, drunken men, but still pressing onwards to throw themselves, without attempt at parrying, upon our bayonets, as the surest way to slay or cut one victim before deaths agony stiffened their limbs … who but could admire and applaud such dauntless bravery?"

A square was a four-sided defensive infantry formation with the front ranks kneeling and presenting bayonets while the rear ranks fired. Having no flanks, it was considered impregnable to infantry or cavalry (though vulnerable to artillery fire); a fully-formed British square had never been broken by assault, and remained so until Abu Klea, some 12 months later. The Black Watch gave Burleigh credit for saving their broken square at Tamaai. Fredrick Villiers, correspondent for The Graphic, recalled hearing Burleighs voice above the din saying, " Give it to the beggars, let 'em have it boys! Hurrah. Three cheers – Hurrah!" and believed that many a man who had feared the day lost rallied on that cheer. Through the struggle the voice of Burleigh was heard when other voices could not be distinguished. He did some fighting, but his goal was to prevent panic, hold the men and get them reformed.

General Bullers Brigade pushed up and launched a withering crossfire causing the enemy to begin to thin, and when the reformed lines began to push back, he felt a little ashamed as they all (he included) laughed and cheered; "that's the way. Give it them men!" Nearly every man present at the battle had a narrow escape at some time, and all who took part could speak of little else but the events of that day for weeks. War, he added was "murderous, cruel at best wherever I have seen it, no matter whether black or white, savage or civilised man engages in it. Where a war is not dictated by stern duty or necessity, it is absolutely devoid of redeeming feature, except the hardihood and bravery with which some men sacrifice their lives". Burleigh estimated about 100 British killed and 2400 enemy.

The reformed brigades eventually won through to the top of the ridge. In the valley of Tamaai below, the huts and tents of Digna's camp came into view; there were very few people about, most either having been killed or having swiftly retreated, leaving stores and ammunition scattered about, the town was later burnt to the ground. After the days fighting, whilst surveying the town, Burleigh felt most proud, he caught up with General Graham, the commander and asked him if the fighting was over for the day, to which he replied in the affirmative, Burleigh said he was going to head to the wire at Suakim; it was 11.40am, and the General at once began to write his brief despatch announcing victory, confirming numbers of dead and wounded with Burleigh, and handing it to him; he was the only civilian to ever be asked by a general to carry his despatches. Burleigh galloped off straight to the town; there were plenty of trophies in the field he would have like to have taken, spears, knives and shields, but riding at 14 stone, and as speed was everything he decided he could not afford to handicap himself. He met several Arabs on the way, but circumnavigated them, ready to gallop on if he had to. He reached Suakim at 2pm, and being a dutiful correspondent tried to get his message off first. The telegraph operators had their orders and with bad grace, Burleigh yielded and gave the generals telegram first, shortly followed by his own messages, which he wrote out in the telegraph office.

The following chapters in Burleighs campaign book highlight the general comments and criticisms he heard around camp from all quarters, these types of summary were obviously an important part of his job; all were general recommendations that could be taken into account for future battles and to gauge public opinion back home. They included aspects and recommendations regarding intelligence gathering, the amount of water needed per man, better maps and the use of local guides. Burleigh also noted the weakness of the British bayonets and swords which would buckle on coming into contact with the bone. the Arabs weapons did not do this and the Arabs themselves were superior in their use of such weapons.

Back at Suakim, the troops were rested, and a warrant was put out for Osman Digna, the friendly sheiks got together with the British representatives, and it was decided they could only open up trade routes by working together. The British did not want to occupy the lands, but it was felt they may have to fight again in order to ensure the safe withdrawal of trapped garrisons. Burleigh himself returned to his lodgings in Mr Levi's, returning to his routine of visits to forts and men to find out what may happen, occasionally he left the town for a ride, a bit of exploring and hunting. On one hunting trip Burleigh went out with a couple of Lieutenants from the Mounted Infantry; they followed the path of what was presumed, through the African heat haze to be a camp fire, it turned out to be a seam of quartz jutting out of a mountain side. On the trip they encountered gazelle and bustards, but they only managed to bag an antelope; the Lieutenant had lost his horse so Burleigh gave him his whilst he went to despatch the animal, he soon realised he was alone on the plain and did not feel it was good place to be so he grabbed the animal by the horns and started to make his way back to camp; after a couple of miles the heat started to get to him and luckily his rather bemused and worried comrades found him and they got back to camp safely.

Despite his defeats, Osman Digna was still resisting British control, and the Arabs themselves declared peace was unlikely if the Egyptians were left to govern the country, as they had proved their military superiority over them. The British took on a small hunt for Digna around Tamaai, but apart from a few minor skirmishes, there was little to report, except that Burleigh who had went on ahead of a skirmish line, came face to face with an Arab who took a point blank shot at him from 90 yards, but missed! It was decided that to find Digna was like finding a needle in a haystack, and an end to the campaign was soon ordered. Burleigh hoped that Digna's power was now sufficiently eroded as he had run into the hills without offering battle. At around this time, Digna wrote to Burleigh directly with an invitation to join the true believers, perhaps, because Burleigh had recently personally saved Digna's nephew after he had been shot. As time passed, all that was left to do was for Burleigh to chronicle the last of the movements around Suakim, shake the dust out of his clothes, pockets and watch-case and head home via Lower Egypt along with the last of the troops.

Burleighs chronicle, Desert Warfare, finishes with a supplementary chapter; "Can Gordon be saved?" which is the copy of a letter by the Telegraphs Special Correspondent regarding General Gordon's deteriorating situation in Khartoum; the narrative of his well-being had the nation on tenterhooks at the time. General Gordon, the Governor General of the Sudan had been held under siege in Khartoum by the Mahdists for some time, when after much debate, the Government decided to send out a relief force. Burleigh suggested the way to save him and his men was to build a railway from Suakim to Berber, arguing that the Mahdi's followers would desert him once they saw the British taking firm control of the land, and, if they could save Gordon they would surely end the African slave trade for ever.

Lord Wolseley's recalled in his Gordon relief campaign journal, that on October 8th 1884, Burleigh and some other correspondents had started to amass for the campaign around Alexandria. They complained to Lord Wolseley and their respective papers that censorship and delays in sending forward telegrams meant it was useless to send anymore. Lord Wolseley had no love of the press, and Burleigh in particular, describing them as "high toned Gentlemen" partly because they denounced his strategy and also, because after any fight they were happy to lay down the law on any military subject and condemn any officer without hesitation to the populous back home. Perhaps, the Crimean war artist, Simpson, summed up this side of the profession the best when he said, that "If the correspondent blames anyone, or any body of men, in the performance of duty, he is hated. If he praises any one there are always others who consider they have done equally well … and they abuse the correspondent for not noticing their merits. Of course, those who are praised, are very friendly to the correspondent. The result is that the correspondent is much courted and much hated."

As the men headed up the Nile for General Gordon's relief, Sir Alfred Turner, recalls a meeting with Bennet Burleigh in his memoirs. On 1st December 1884, at a place called Akhashieh, on the banks of the Nile, his party were preparing their bivouac when they heard a strange rattling noise some distance away across the water. They soon discovered a man making his way to the bank, he made his way ashore, and Turner was surprised to see it was Bennet Burleigh. His boat had been wrecked and sunk, and he was rattling the oars to keep the swarming crocodiles at bay, he managed to save himself by swimming a considerable distance to the bank. He adds, "this was one of the very many remarkable escapes from death of Mr Bennet Burleigh, who has been more often in close contact with that, so represented, horrible spectre than anyone I know". Burleigh had lost everything expect his money which was in a pocket in his belt. Sir Turner went on to give him a set of clothes and some provisions which were gratefully received. He never expected to see the clothes again, but one day towards the end of the campaign he received a parcel contain all the lent apparel, they were slightly grimy having been worn at Abu Klea and Metemmeh, but at that late stage of the campaign when clothing was short, Burleighs conscientious thoughts were most appreciated. Major General Adye also recounts this incident in his memoirs, adding that the war correspondent Frederick Villiers was also a passenger of the boat, and that the touch of slapping oars to fend off the crocodiles was actually pure Daily Telegraph! The General lunched with them a few hours later at Korti, and believed them worse for wear; he supplied Villiers with some art materials to replace those which he had lost. Lord Wolseley also recounts this event in his campaign journal, though his anti correspondent opinion, which he justifies, is not so favourable to Burleigh, but he was very much amused when he heard the story. He claims that Burleigh had sponged a meal off a Major Barrow and his detachment of Hussars whilst camping at Sarras. Burleigh had his own boat and said he would meet them again the next evening at Semmeh. According to Wolseley, the soldiers were relieved that they would be rid of Burleigh as he would not be able to travel as far as them that day, but astonishingly Burleigh did arrive at their camp that evening, where "of course he again drew upon their hospitality; although he swaggered about living on 9 dates a day, he pitched into their food with vengeance. He had carried away his rudder and his mast; his sailing gear was all in a bad way. He gaily asked Barrow if their were any Hussars who were sore from riding as he would gladly take a few to Dongola in his boat - good natured man! He wanted them to pull him and his boat there. His crew consisted of a pilot, one boy and himself. Barrow and he parted. The following day I think it was that Burleigh with nothing on but a pair of canvas trousers was seen on the bank of the river scraping a hole deep enough to bury his pilot. His boat was wrecked, went down and he lost the few things he had with him, the pilot being drowned. As he covered up the pilots body with sand he was heard to say 'I don't wish to say anything ill of the dead, but this was all his fault.' A day afterwards he appeared clothed again, having begged things I suppose off those whom he met. He is a real good beggarman. This begging talent is a very necessary one for the regular out-and-out newspaper correspondent and is one of the reasons why it is so difficult for a Gentleman to serve in that capacity where he is pitted against men who are not bound by certain generally accepted canons of honour. To rival Billy Russell or Forbes, you must be utterly indifferent to truth and prepared to fawn upon those who will either give you dinner or information and who will not scruple to bribe servants, telegraph and other clerks and to 'jump' a horse or pony when you require them. This man Mr Burleigh begged sugar, tea and coffee etc. from the Quarter Master 19th Hussars before starting on his journey which ended so unfortunately for him."

Shortly after this time, a bit further up the Nile in Debbeh, Burleigh and a servant, in search of news and adventure had entered the territory without authorisation. Here he had a chance meeting with Captain Kitchener, as he was then. Burleigh was the first white man Kitchener had seen in weeks and he was glad to catch up on the news. The pair got to know each other well. Kitchener generally detested journalists, found them a liability to intelligence, and "drunken swabs", with a few rare exceptions, Burleigh being one of them; the feeling was mutual, Burleigh was almost humbled by Kitcheners great leadership in the Sudan. Although it is reputed Burleigh did not drink, in the middle of Debbeh,

Kitchener managed to produce two bottles of claret, which the two drank at dinner. Another version of this meeting transcribed by Chesterton, recalls Burleigh wandering freely near Dongola and getting into conversation with an Arab who spoke excellent English, this Arab turned out to be Kitchener, in Arab dress and fluent in the native tongue, so convincing was he that his blue eyes did not give him away to Burleigh.

The main Gordon relief column made slow progress up the Nile, eventually reaching Gakdul Wells, and two days later, they encountered a large Mahdist army, about 3 miles from the Abu Klea Wells. All through the night before the battle of Abu Klea, January 17th 1885, the enemy chanted and played the tom-toms, and intermittently fired their Remington rifles from the low hill to the front of General Stewarts camp, where 1800 men lay wrapped in their blankets, sleeping with their guns, bayonets fixed, firmly to hand. Before dawn there were several alarms which brought the whole force to their feet.

During the earlier part of the night, Burleigh and others were talking with one of Britain's most famous officers of the age, Colonel Fred Burnaby, who told them of his satisfaction at having arrived in time for the approaching battle. Burnaby wasn't supposed to be there as headquarters would have forbidden him, but he felt the need for another daring adventure. Burleigh and Burnaby had first met in 1882, when Burnaby made his attempt to be the first man to cross the English Channel by hot air balloon, the Telegraph suggested that Burleigh accompany him, but Burnaby wanted, and got the glory all for himself. Shortly afterwards, on a Saturday, Burleigh bumped into a Mr Wright who was on his way to visit Burnaby and review the account of his voyage that he had written for the publishers, Burleigh asked Mr Wright to introduce them, which he did later that day, though little was exchanged between the men, as Burnaby had promised his publisher to divulge no information.

However, come the Monday morning, a detailed account of the journey appeared in the Telegraph, and it was not told how Burleigh had got the information, but it was an accomplished feat for a young man just starting out in his career. Sometime later, at the house of Telegraphs proprietor, Lord Burnham, the pair struck up a warm friendship. Another meeting was later noted, on 1st June 1884 there was a party to celebrate the opening of the new Daily Telegraph offices on Fleet Street; some 600 people were invited, including the Prince of Wales, various Lords, Dukes,

Ambassadors, and leading figures in law, science and society. Amongst the members of the services was Col Fred Burnaby, who spent the evening talking with Burleigh.

After the battle, Burleigh was to learn that Burnaby had been appointed as second in command by General Wolseley, and would later have been made Governor of Metamneh. The evenings conversation continued by the hour, joking and laughing - On politics, Burnaby championed the Tory cause and Burleigh, the Social Democratic; indeed, General Stewart, more than once, asked them to be silent. "Where's your double-barrelled shot gun?" inquired Burleigh of Burnaby.
"Oh," was the reply. "As the sentimentalists and their friends at home made such an outcry on account of my using it at El Teb, I have handed it over to my servant."
"That was a mistake," said Burleigh, "… These cruel devils of Dervishes give no quarter…. it's their lives or ours."
"It is too late now," said Burnaby. "I must take my chance"

The next morning at 9.30 the British square advanced, only to be confronted by 4 or 5 thousand of the Mahdist troops, "like a vast wave of black surf, their white teeth shining and their arms flashing like thousands of mirrors". Burleigh goes on to describe the fall of Burnaby, and the following passage, though edited from the original, shows the power of his writing. He says he observed all of Burnaby's actions during the battle from about thirty yards, he "rode out in front of the rear of the left face, apparently to assist two or three of our skirmishers … he put himself in the way of a sheikh charging down on horseback … {a bullet or Burnaby's sword,} brought the sheikh headlong to the ground. The enemy's spearmen were close behind and one of them suddenly dashed at Colonel Burnaby, pointing the long blade of his spear at his throat. Checking his horse, … Burnaby … parried the Muslim's rapid and ferocious thrusts … The affray was the work of three or four seconds only … the scene was taken in at a glance - with that lightning instinct which I have seen the desert warriors before now display in battle while coming to one another's aid - by an Arab who, pursuing a soldier, had passed five paces to Burnaby's right and rear. Turning with a sudden spring, this second Arab ran his spear into the Colonels right shoulder. It was a slight wound - enough though to cause Burnaby to twist around … brief as was Burnaby's glance backwards … it was long enough to enable the first Arab to deliver his spear point full in the brave officers throat {a second blow caused him to come off his horse} … half a dozen Arabs were now about him. With the blood gushing in streams from his gashed throat, the dauntless Guardsman leapt to his feet, sword in hand, and slashed at the ferocious group. They were the wild strokes of a proud, brave man dying hard."

Burleigh continued to describe the battle, "The charge of the Arabs carried many of them into the centre of our square, ... There death and havoc rioted for two or three minutes, whilst our men moved off from the inextricable mass of wounded, dying, and dead camels. It was awful scene, for many alas! Of the wounded left behind ... perished by the hands of the merciless Arabs ... {who} ran hither and thither thirsting for blood." Burleigh continues, showing us he was not afraid of joining in himself, "At this stage, seeing the Arabs were no respecters of person, I myself took up a Martini-Henry, but the third cartridge stuck, and I had to resort to my revolver." The battle ended as the British who were clustered around a circular mound, kept backing up until they were wedged into a compact mass, the position enabling them to deliver a heavy and withering fire for ten minutes or so into the dense mass of Arabs. The enemy soon wavered, two or three at first, then twenties and fifties began to trot off the field. After five minutes it was over, the British had lost 100 with 200 wounded, the enemy about 500-600, maybe even twice that.

Two days later, the next battle took place at Abu Kru, General Stewart had decided to set up camp about 4 miles from the Nile. Just before the battle, the correspondents, Burleigh, Pearse and Prior, whose written stories were burning holes in their pockets, and together doubting their chances of survival in the upcoming battle, decided to risk it across the desert. However Prior had come to the conclusion that the game was already up and that their only true chance of survival was a ride for life to the rear. Before they mounted their horses they shook hands and swore that they would get through or die together. If one was wounded the others were to stand by him to the death. They mounted their horses and rode off, quietly at first. They rode through a small forest, and then speeded up. The going was good, until Burleigh said, "there is a line of skirmishes in front, and once we get through them we are all right.". They got through at a gallop as bullets rained around them. However, they then spotted some cavalry, and realising they had made a dreadful mistake, and seeing the impossibility of the situation, they returned back to the square; given their speed, some of the British soldiers, presuming they were fanatical Arabs riding such a gallop, nearly shot them. The men had been lucky as all of their horses had been hit.

That morning, at 7 a.m. the enemy opened up from a range of about 1400 yards and the British soldiers were pummelled by shot, everything was done to try and induce the enemy to come closer but to no avail, and the battle lasted seven hours. A kind of fort was ordered to be built in the middle distance out of meat and biscuit boxes in order to protect the troops. Lord Dundonald was in charge of the operation, and Bennet Burleigh, most energetic with advice, lent a willing hand. Burleigh took command of 40 officers and men, all were volunteers for a task which seemingly meant certain death. Thanks to his leading role in the building of these defences, under fire, Burleigh was mentioned in despatches. It was at this spot, some time later, while giving instructions and examining the enemy's position, that General Stewart received his mortal wound in the groin.

During this battle, Burleigh was hit twice, once in the neck and once in the foot. According to the war artist, Melton Prior, he was chatting with Burleigh when he heard a tremendous thud. Burleigh yelled 'Pick it out, Prior! Pick it out!' at the same time clawing at his neck. Prior looked and replied, ' there is nothing to pick out.',' Pick it out, idiot!' - "Surely enough a ricochet bullet had struck Burleigh in the muscle just under the ear, and soon raised a great black lump half the size of a chicken's egg, but the shock and pain was so great that he would not believe me that there was nothing to pick out. He was soon pacified, however."

All the correspondents in the field that day save one received a bullet. One of the correspondents, James Cameron, was sitting between camels eating sardines and biscuit when he received a fatal bullet at about 10a.m..The following morning the correspondents decided they would bury Cameron themselves. Burleigh, Prior, Pearce and Villiers carried him to the mass burial pit that had already been dug, here they placed him with their own hands, and a burial service was read for him and the other casualties of the battle that day interred.

On the 19th January, Colonel Marling V.C. made an entry in his diary, in which he remarks "Sankey Herbert was shot through the head dead about 1p.m. Bennet Burleigh, … and I buried him about 2.30p.m., at least we got two Tommies to scratch a shallow hole in the sand and covered him up. He had on a pair of new brown field boots, which he got at the last post before we left Korti. Bennet Burleigh wanted to take these boots, as his own were worn out, and he said it was a sin to waste a good pair of boots on a dead man. I, being young and more squeamish in those days, protested, and said, "Damn it, Burleigh, you cant take the boots off poor old Sankey", and so we buried him. Next day, when we came back from Metemmeh to pick up the wounded, and stores, and camels, I passed the spot where we had buried Sankey, and there were his poor old feet in a pair of Tommy's grey socks sticking out of the sand. When I saw Burleigh about two hours afterwards, he had on a new pair of field boots which, however, were too tight for his fat calves, and he had slit them up behind." This anecdote is a good reflection of Burleighs experience in the battlefield as the author later went on to remark that both the officers and men's boots were all in a sorry state, and that he doubted there were a dozen spare pairs in the whole column. Times were tough, all the men suffered having to camp out in exposed conditions, it was 90 degrees Fahrenheit in the shade at noon, with a northerly a wind that would smoother you in dust. A typical night spent in luxury would involve four stakes hammered in the ground of a depression out of the wind, covered on three sides and overhead by spare blankets and sacking; however, such conditions made Burleigh an inventive man, for his life in the field, he developed a bed on a concertina principle which could be thrown on the ground, and pulled out, and when a mattress and mosquito net were added it guaranteed a good nights sleep and when it was collapsed, it turned into a handy suitcase, into which all sorts of things could be packed.

In the square at Abu Kru, there were said to be less than a thousand men against 10 times that number, but the square held, the foe were thrown back three times, and finally routed. At the end of battle Burleigh and Prior helped carry the wounded to the new camp on the Nile. During this campaign, Burleigh distinguished himself not only as a correspondent but also by volunteering his services in the trenches and in carrying despatches.

The battles and the British advance all seemed to be in vain, A relief force of 240 men was sent forward towards Khartoum, but contact between them and General Gordon was precarious. Through this entire period, the despatches of Burleigh were widely read with intense interest. To quote The Daily Telegraph, " all Christendom turned its eyes to that lonely Englishman, Gordon, at Khartoum."

A week or so later, after the main relief force took part in the Battle of Gubat, the news came in that the Mahdi had taken Khartoum and that General Gordon, an "icon of his age", had been slain (26th January 1885).

Burleigh described the feeling amongst the soldiers; "On all sides, among officers and men, there was universal dismay and indignation at the catastrophe". Burleigh then rode through hostile territory to Dongola, and wired the news of Gordon's death back to London, for which the Telegraph got a world wide scoop.

The anxiety of the British public was now focused on the chances of the relief force making a safe retreat as the Mahdi's men were planning to cut them off. On Saturday February 21st 1885 the Daily Telegraph pointed out the dire straits of the force up the Nile which sent the British public into a panic. However, in the early hours of February 22nd, Burleigh once again got to the wire first, and after filing his message that the force was safe, in order to give it a head start, he continued to occupy this only wire with trivia. His message therefore, not only beat those of his fellow correspondents, but also the official despatch by 24 hours. On hearing that the column had reached a place of safety, The Telegraph was then determined to do an unheard-of thing for them and release a Sunday edition, and on their way to Sunday service, the population read the good news, which was a scoop for this special Sunday edition and which Burleigh later listed as his proudest moment in journalism.

As a war correspondent, Burleigh also had a very important role of influence amongst the public and government. For instance, in May 1885, when the campaign was almost over, Burleigh reported that there was something wrong with the quality of the weapons used by the British soldier and issued a full condemnation of the cartridges, swords and bayonets. He said, " the triangular bayonets offtimes bent and twisted", and the"… complex ill shaped boxer cartridge was the cause of most of the jamming that occurred…Many a soldier at Abu Klea saw with dismay his bayonet rendered useless at the moment where there was no chance to load his rifle."

In a similar vein, on another occasion, Burleigh embarrassed the War office in his denouncement of the bullets of the Lee-Metford Rifle; "the War Office authorities have reams of correspondence on the valueless character of the Lee-Metford rifle bullet. Indeed, the rifle itself has come in for severe strictures, as being inferior in its magazine arrangement to the German and Italian weapons; whilst the cordite is described as "an indifferent explosive compared to the powder of other countries." However, all that may be, certainly the soldiers have no faith in the stopping qualities of the Lee-Metford bullet. Under superior orders, issued at Dekesh camp, large details from each regiment were engaged daily in filing off the tips of the Lee-Metford bullet. One million rounds had to be so dealt with. They were doing the same thing in the Cairo arsenal. It is little short of a scandal that an army in the field has to sit down whilst the men re-make its ammunition".

Burleighs concerns inflamed the publics concern, which prompted official inquiries and questions in Parliament; These, and stories like them were reprinted in many newspapers, and through such persistence the efficiency and weapons of the British Army were improved.

For his role in the Gordon relief expedition, Burleigh won the honour courted by all soldiers, a mention in the official despatches by order of the Commander in Chief, for magnificent heroism in the building of the defensive wall, the first time that honour was extended to a correspondent. and it is said that if the conditions under which the Victoria Cross were awarded would have allowed it to be given to a civilian, Burleigh would have been thus honoured with one.

Khartoum had fallen, and the Sudan and its people were abandoned by the British who set the Egyptian border at Wadi Halfa. The Mahdis own successes in Khartoum killed him within six months as he yielded to a life of indolence and lust. His successor, Abdullah the Taaishi, or the Khalifa was far more ignorant and cruel than his dead master; he had visions of founding a new empire; he ruled with a ruthless, barbarous and fanatical tyranny, which caused his allied tribes to fall away from his rule and return to orthodox Islam. Omdurman remained the Dervish capital with some 30,000 soldiers in its vicinity, the strongest native military power North Africa had ever known. It was not until the following year that the British Government seriously looked at reconquering Sudan, starting with the reoccupation of Dongola in order to protect the new railway line which would solve the huge problems of transporting troops and their supplies around the Sudan.

Part B - The road to Omdurman

Burleigh who had thus far been present at all of the campaigns in the Sudan in which the British troops were involved, returned to Egypt several years later in 1897 in order to be on hand should a sudden dash be made for Khartoum due to some lapse in power of the Mahdi's successor, the Khalifa. The charge would be led by the Sirdar (Kitchener was appointed Sirdar in 1892), a Hindustani word which originally meant leader or possessor. Burleigh himself argued that it remained for the latter part of the century to see orderly government and the extension of civilisation under European control in the Sudan, rather than the "horrible rule by savagery … where property and life are at the instant disposal of passion and the sword."

Due to the years of oppressive conditions imposed on the people, Khalifa Abdullah's rule was under threat. In the north of the country occupation by both the Egyptians and British was increasing. The Khedival troops (soldiers of the rulers of Egypt) were planning to take over the south eastern town of Kassala from the Italians due to a border change , and thinking this seemed to be the best chance of a good story, that is where Burleigh headed. Once again his journey began at Suakim which, after years of hardship, was enjoying a renewed prosperity and security thanks to its occupation by the Khedival troops.

As Christmas was approaching, Burleigh became anxious to leave Suakim for Kassala, via Tokar and along the old postal route so he quickly made the transport arrangements to take a trip that no European had made for over 14 years; however, the Sirdar refused him permission so he decided to go by sea to Massowah, and through the Italian colony of Eritrea. The military authorities put no obstacle in his way with regard to travelling this route, and as no steamer was making the journey for a month, he hired a native sambuk to cover the 300 miles. He left Suakin for Massowah on November 13th in rather windy conditions, knowing that he had to set off regardless, as his rivals had heard of his trip and hired a much faster dhow. Despite its appearances, the sambuk held up magnificently well in the poor weather; however, after four hours, it was decided to secure shelter in the lee of a coral islet for the night and make repairs; Burleigh disembarked to explore, picking through shells and inspecting bird nests, then he took a somewhat cautious bath in the shallows being somewhat concerned with the local shark population. The crew set sail again the following morning pleased that the bed sharing rats on board had not disembarked, which was a good sign according to the sailors. They eventually landed at the prosperous port of Massowah on the morning of the third day where provisions were collected and transport arranged, they departed on an inland train that same afternoon. After taking dinner at the end of the line, Burleigh, his servant and guides set out in the dark and rain on the first stage of their overland journey. Throughout the night the men and mules clambered through rocky passes seen only by the gleaming eyes of the predators they spotted through the darkness. Eventually, they stumbled into the town of Gindah at five in the morning; completely exhausted having covered a distance of 25 miles. Burleigh slept in the local Greek café until 9am, had some breakfast, exchanged mules, and resumed the journey. Further on, they scaled the great mountain plateau of Abyssinia, one of the most picturesque, novel and interesting trips Burleigh claims he had ever made, not stopping until they reached Asmara at 5pm. After a week of long days and more than a few wildlife encounters the adventurous journey ended with a camp near the Italian fort on the plains of Kassala. The city was somewhat rundown, Burleigh joked that Hyenas were more common in Kassala than dogs were on Clapham Common! Despite the fact that the Hyenas were a cowardly sort, many a nights sleep was lost due to their pack howling. Burleigh stayed in the Italian fort and found the soldiers most agreeable companions and immensely enjoyed their nightly arias. Being the first Englishman in the area for many years, Burleigh himself was somewhat of a curiosity, particularly among the females who would flirt with him by displaying their jewellery and other charms. Towards Christmas 1897, the Italians welcomed the incoming Anglo-Egyptian troops with open arms and a full handover of the territory took place on Christmas Day, putting an end to the last remnants of Mahdism in the Eastern Sudan.

Burleigh enjoyed his stay in Kassala, but soon headed back to Suakim, on this journey they slept in the presence of sniffing lions and leopards; he mentions that he had many adventures on his trip home through the Abyssinian mountains, but unfortunately, as his book is a narrative of war, he does not divulge the details. After this grand tour, he returned to London via Cairo in the early days of 1898 where he expected to spend several months at home.

The homecoming didn't last long however, as important threatening events were starting to take place, and when, after only a few days at home, the Khalifa began to amass his armies 18 miles north of Omdurman, Burleigh set off back down the Nile. The followers of the Mahdi and Khalifa became known to the outside world as the Dervish, they themselves preferred to be called "Ansar" which means "helper"; the original Ansar helped the prophet Mohammed when he was in exile, and the actual Dervish were simply Muslim Friars who had taken a vow of poverty and austerity.

The Sirdar had sought to dispense with the attendance of war correspondents once and for all by imposing unusual conditions and allowing them to travel no further south than Aswan. There was naturally a huge outcry from all quarters, and within 24 hours the regulation was repealed, allowing travel to the rail head at Wady Halfa. Burleigh was later told by Lord Cromer that the order had been in the interests of the newspapers in order to save them money, but added that the "…editors did not exercise enough care in making their selection of representatives, and unfit men were often sent out, who did much harm in many ways"

Once the correspondents reached Wadi Halfa, they set up their tents within the armies camp, and watched as huge amounts of goods and troops moved in to the area and then out again to the more southerly town of Berber. During his stay in this camp Burleigh wrote about the general goings on, such as the excellent training and condition of the men, the prohibition of alcohol, the poor rations of food, and the inferior bullets of the Lee Metford rifle, a million of which were having to have their tips filed down to increase their stopping abilities.

The Khalifa meanwhile was also pushing his troops north to the town of Metemneh. The atmosphere at camp became electric with excitement, conflict was looming. Burleigh managed to catch the train South to Dekesh camp near Abu Hamed and Kitchener made the correspondents and other followers pay for their tickets; Burleigh however saw this as admirable; the Sirdar had conducted some of the cheapest campaigns on record. However, as luck would have it, the correspondents couldn't travel as the railway was overburdened with the demands of the army.

The British rail gangs were completing up to 2 miles of track a day so, in early February the troops moved 18 miles on, to the new railhead at Abu Dis, rather than Berber itself, as the railhead camps were easier for keeping the men supplied. This camp was also chosen because it was thought that the troops would be stuck here for quite a while, and that the men would benefit from its close proximity to the Nile and its more pleasant surrounds. Burleigh headed back to Wady Halfa in order to see after his own transport, and on 28th February, the correspondents received permission to go onward to Berber. The correspondents had been forbidden to hire camels from natives, so Burleigh and an artist friend, (probably Prior), had to procure several donkeys for their luggage and were even lucky enough to find a donkey that could take Burleighs weight.

During this journey to Berber, in which the men ended up walking most of the way anyway, the Correspondents bumped into some Arabs who hired them some camels. The journey was still slow going and they did not reach Berber in time for the 10.30pm admittance cut off, en route they spotted an empty house, and on entering the spacious enclosure, they struck a light, being horrified to find about eight armed Arabs in various states of repose, luckily the men were friendlies, so the fire was built up and sleep undertaken. The men woke at 2am and soon set off arriving in Berber at around sunrise. A colonel treated them to soap and a bath followed by a splendid breakfast and lunch, the first good meals they had had in days. During the afternoon the men secured a detached and clean, but bare mud house to live in with the animals being secured in the adjacent compound. The men had little to grumble about and were quite glad they did not have to live in the town proper with its shocking sanitary and disease breeding conditions. Apart from the dirt, life in Berber was still a bit of a burden, the post office was three miles away, staffed by a clerk with no English and there was also a pesky black fly that drew blood and rose sores. Burleigh himself found it difficult to believe that the Khalifa could advance at all, and thought perhaps that he was deluding himself. However, his forecast was wrong and the Khalifa started to move his forces north on 12th March heading for the fortified lines of the Egyptian troops at Atbara hoping to eventually destroy the railway, thus strengthening his power. During this time Burleigh made a hasty trip to see and report on the different Anglo-Egyptian camps between Berber and Atbara, he decide to travel by the Nile, saving his livestock for more pressing use, and remembered the several escapes from drowning and other adventures he had had on its waters. This trip however went well, lots of bird life and very few raiding parties and crocodiles! Once back at Berber, he speedily set out again with the British Brigade which had been ordered to Kunar; this time he travelled with all his camels, horses, servants and provisions. Three brigades now lay at Kunar, the Sirdar could now choose to help the Atbara camp or hit the Khalifa's flank if he decided to attack an unprotected Berber; expectations in camp were running high. The plan was to let the Khalifa and his men come to the British across the Atbara Desert unmolested, the British would then fall on and pursue them, thus ensuring very few made it back from whence they came.

Come March 20th the whole British force was marched out to the Atbara Desert following the suspected path of the Khalifa's men. The Atbara itself marked the dividing line between tropical and subtropical Sudan in so far as wild animals are concerned, to the south large prey and hence larger predators were much more prolific. The march was a dust laden affair, the heat and dust were ever present problems in the Sudan; Burleigh describes an encounter with a sand devil; "The 'devil', small or large, is a whirlwind that spins and skips across the desert, marking his course by a column of sand, dust and pebbles. He is brother to the ocean waterspout and often as mischievous and dangerous. Three of them waltzed in close succession through the Egyptian and British lines. They came to us across the desert, in appearance mighty, inverted, whirling black cones, their points from 40 to 80 feet in diameter. When they struck the camp it was with a roar as of many rushing trains in a tunnel. As they furiously spun, coats, blankets, helmets, papers, bully beef tins, in sooth, all the flotsam and jetsam of the camp within reach, were caught up in the ascending vortex, and borne as bubbles to the clouds. Tents and tukels went as they sidled by, and the brave Camerons and Seaforths had great work with their kilts. When the devils were gone, we all were as black as sweeps, and almost blinded and choked with grit and sand". During the march, and in the subsequent camp, there were surprise attacks and skirmishes coming through the bush; one fatal surprise attack occurred during a lunch break, but at least contact had been made with the Dervish and over time, their exact whereabouts and fortifications were confirmed by the scouting parties, whom the correspondents were not allowed to join during this campaign. The men sensed that the day of the battle was coming closer; however it seemed that the Khalifa's men would not be drawn into a fight so soon.

On Monday April 4th, the camp was moved to a temporary camp at Abadar, the idea being to avoid a toilsome march later on, ensuring that the fighting men would be that bit fresher. From this camp, Burleigh sent his groom, who was an ex Egyptian trooper to Dakala in order to send despatches to England; on his trip he had a frightful experience and was chased by some Dervish horsemen, but thanks to his swift stead, he made it in safety to a camp of friendly Arabs. The new camp was only 8 miles from the enemy, and it was known by Thursday 7th April that a battle would take place the following day; As It happened, that day was Good Friday, a Holy Day for the Christians and Muslims within the Sirdars troops. It was a busy day, packing, getting a few days supplies together and letter writing, however, it was forbidden to wire home about the coming event. Around this time Burleigh had a fall one morning when his horses legs were struck from under him, but the delight of going to battle and escaping the monotony of waiting around and weary marches probably speeded up the healing process. By 3pm everything was ready for the advance, and at six in the evening, everybody was in their place to start the march, and a few minutes later, " the glint of pipe or cigarette could be seen here and there in the squares, but beyond that and the heavy trampling of the troops upon sand and gravel, there was nothing to give warning that an army was engaged in that most difficult and risky enterprise, a night march." Dervish scouts were deceived by the camps still burning fires which friendly natives kept alight through the night. "When darkness had quite fallen, all that could be seen was the shadowy outline of the particular square one happened to be with, or the cold shimmer of the bayonets of the next," and " even when the moon rose her light disclosed little more of the movement of the brigades, for there was a fresh breeze stirring, and the sand and dust drove by as thick as a Newfoundland fog."

At 9 p.m. a halt was made in order for food, water and a four hour bivouac. Burleigh, spent this time visiting the troops and observing the Sirdar and his staff in the square. In one of his more amusing observations Burleigh wrote: " it was whilst walking softly, so as not to disturb light sleepers, that I overheard a sentimental Seaforth Highlander say to a comrade:
　' Ah, Tam, how many thousands there are at hame across the sea thinking o' us this nicht!'
　'Right, Sandy,' replied his chum, ' and how many millions there are that don't care a d---. Go to sleep, you fool!'
And silence again fell upon that corner of the square."

Shortly after one in the morning on Good Friday; the men fell into line again. Now there was no smoking or talking, but the rumble of gun carriages could not be hidden. Orders were given by sign language, as the moon now flooded the desert with light. Just before dawn, Burleigh surveyed the camp with field glasses from a knoll, where he spied the Dervish camp fires and flags and the Dervish themselves standing in front of their trenches and forts watching the British and he knew they meant to fight. As the sun rose, there was a great stir in the Dervish camp. Burleigh reported that the Dervish did not come forward to attack, he knew they knew that the British would then have the advantage; "These were no longer mad fanatical Dervishes, believing they had as comrades in arms hosts of beings from the other world fighting by their side, spurring them on to win the joys of the Moslem's paradise". A cannonade of several hours followed, Burleigh joined with Gatacre's brigade. At 8am the bugle call came for a general attack on the entrenched enemy. The Khedival bands and the pipers started to play. As the battle raged from trench to trench no quarter was given or asked; Burleigh, who had managed to get through a gap in the zereba said the battle "was furious and ticklish, as of clearing out by hand a hive of hornets." As the ground was rough, Burleigh was mindful as he mounted his horse to get a better view and as the bullets flew he reminisced; "I several times caught myself wondering when I was going to get the first one. But not even my clothing was caught." As the British approached the inner zereba which was full of 2000 of the Khalifa's specially chosen followers, a rush was made, and some companies were all but annihilated in a storm of bullets; some of the Dervish fled for a last, but brief stand on the banks of the Atbara. By the end of the battle, the British had lost around 500 men, with Burleigh estimating that the enemy had lost an estimated 3000 men, and had as many wounded who were probably going to later die in the desert into which they had fled. The enemies leader Mahmoud was captured alive, but Osman Digna had escaped yet again.

  Burleigh wrote, "After the fatigues of the march and the excitement of the action, and when I had finished despatching my long but hastily written telegrams, which were scrawled out while sitting upon the pebbles under a blazing desert sun, half blinded and wholly wearied, and terribly thirsty and hungry, I managed to procure some refreshment"; the telegrams had been hastily written and despatched but as the censors had not allowed casualty figures to be included, Burleigh complained,"The rules of military censorship did not permit the transmission of my figures... it is perhaps after all a merciful regulation that breaks news of loss and suffering by degrees... I confess that I never like to be the first to wire or write, giving the information of the death of any person... Except in special instances, such as where the public interest overweighs those of the few."

Burleigh followed the troops back to one of the Nile camps, but having been busy writing and sending despatches, he had lost his servants, and accepted an invitation to dinner from the cavalry officers and so was not forced to bivouac hungry and blanketless on the desert floor. The following day he made his way back to Abadar camp, where he met many a Greek trader and native doing a roaring business in small commodities; again he couldn't find his servants and this time ended up sleeping blanketless on the desert floor, he found them the following morning, the rascals having been too busy looting and bartering to care for Burleighs needs. He stayed around camp until after the Sunday church service when he headed back to Dakala, spending the night on a friends boat; he then caught the train back to Cairo in which the Dervish leader Mahmoud was also transported.

During this 36 hour rail journey to Wady Halfa, the two had frequent conversations, Burleigh also took a photograph of Mahmoud with his pocket camera, (see picture), he insisted on dressing smart to look more becoming; the shot is presented in Burleighs book Sirdar and Khalifa. As soon as Burleigh got beyond the jurisdiction of military censorship in Egypt, he wired home an account of the Dervish leaders views of the battle and his experiences. Rene Bull, the war correspondent for "Black and White" describes the events thus; "After Atbara, Mahmoud was sent a prisoner to Egypt, and one of the correspondents of Black and White happened to join the train when it stopped at a wayside station for the purpose of taking in water. Our representative was so fortunate as to recognise the deposed Mahdist General, and travelled with him, and aided by his knowledge of Arabic succeeded in holding a very long and interesting conversation with the prisoner. The topic most discussed was naturally the recent campaign, more especially in regard to the defence of the zeriba. Our correspondent showed Mahmoud a plan of the battle he had made, and Mahmoud appeared greatly amused at it. He said that the scheme of defence therein suggested was quite wrong, and promptly asked for a piece of paper and pencil, with the aid of which he drew a plan of his defences as originally laid down, with the names of the different Emirs who were charged with the guarding of the various points, written in Arabic." The plan was reproduced in Bull's book about Omdurman, and "affords a very curious and interesting example of semi - barbaric military science".

The final series of events for the possession of the Sudan were soon at hand. Burleigh returned to England for a short time but was back in Cairo by July for the march to Khartoum. During this break, a period of less than three months, his book based on the events at Atbara, "Sirdar and Khalifa", was finished and ready for press.

Part C – Reconquering the Sudan

After the rather unexpected contact at Atbara, it seemed that the Khalifa would not risk sending anymore troops north to confront the British; so the Sirdar sent his troops to summer rest camps in dry, mimosa shaded spots on the banks of the Nile. The troops did the occasional march and used up the million or so "bad" Lee Metford bullets they had previously had to file down for target practice. The British wanted to be ready to push South and end the Khalifa's rule come July, when the Nile is at its highest, allowing the easier passage of both gun and store boats to within 30 miles of Omdurman, where the Khalifa had recalled his best men and where he meant to give battle.

In early July 1898, Burleigh headed to Cairo; here he watched a morning demonstration of the new siege guns that were to be used in levelling the walls and defences of Omdurman which he concluded to be a worthwhile addition to the British army. There was now an open door policy on the numbers of correspondents allowed to the front, provided they could pay £50 for their official permit, plus railway fares and any forage they may require from the stores. Burleigh thought that a few of the correspondents travelling represented anything but, and were more interested in using the name of a newspaper as a cover for notoriety and medal hunting. Burleigh started his journey from Cairo travelling by train, a trip he had undertaken many times before; it took forty hours to reach Aswan; the carriages were dirty, hot and stuffy and had no refreshment car; he had brought his own provisions, but the water became too hot to drink and the too food dusty, he found the journey hateful. The same afternoon he arrived in Aswan, he and three other correspondents, accompanied by a number of Royal Army Medical Corps officers departed on barge number 9 to Wadi Halfa (see picture), where he spent many days watching the huge numbers of new troops arriving.

From Wadi Halfa the men then caught the train, travelling in a horse box, along the new line commissioned by the Sirdar to the Atbara camp; Burleigh thought this line was a stroke of military genius, as it would run all the way to Khartoum when eventually completed thus securing the whole country for the Empire. Upon reaching the camp, the correspondents found they had been sited in a terrible spot, the ground being a light loam that penetrated everything and in the oppressive heat, they were also sheltered from the relief of the rivers breeze; For the two weeks Burleigh spent there, he feared this camps memory would plague him for years and describes his time as "I persisted in existing".

PRESS BARGE NO.9 – ON ROUTE FOR KHARTOUM – BURLEIGH FRONT RIGHT

At Dakhala, also known as the Atbara camp, Burleigh frequently saw and conversed with the Sirdar, generals and officers, they discussed weapons and tactics and he also discovered from them that the British would be in front of Omdurman in a little over a month on one of two dates from August 1st; though it turned out that it would be neither of these dates. The press censor, although courteous, obeyed his orders as to what information could and could not be telegraphed home; but as the censor was also a Colonel with other responsibilities, when more and more copy started to come in from the press men, tempers became frayed and accusations flew as to what was and what was not allowed through. Burleigh thought this system could be improved, and that the British people had a right to know what was going on in the field. He was sympathetic to the idea of censorship, though felt it pointless, as any enemy worth its salt would have lots of spies anyway.

Whilst at the Atbara camp, although correspondents were not allowed to go any great distance, they still got bits of news, such as skirmishes and land grabs on the peripheries of the campaign, their time and copy were also filled with reports on brigade field days, their practice formations and associated drills.

Having obtained permission from headquarters to go to the front, camp was struck on August 15th, the servants, horses and camels were gathered and the gear packed; all was ready to march 140 miles overland with the troops. There was much merry making that night by those due to march; and eventually they settled into their bivouacs on the low scrub by the Nile. Burleigh himself had had dinner with some officer friends. There was a wind storm and a downpour during the night causing the Nile to burst its banks, and many a drenched soldier had to relocate himself quickly; after a nights broken sleep, the first column got away at 6am, but the latter columns not until 8am - which was too late really given the heat of the Sudan during the day. The march itself became disorganised and there were many stragglers, some of whom got lost. Burleigh felt for them as it reminded him of the many lonely nights he too had spent alone in the desert. On one occasion he set up his bivouac in the desert and was eating his dinner by candlelight, when two lost Lancers approached, he fed them and set off with them in the morning. Burleigh and the servants were glad of their company as they were in an area known to be frequented by marauding bandits. The main body of troops then followed the river as they watched the gunboats heading south; Burleigh was an old hand at all this, and he commented that there were only 15 people on this current campaign who had been involved in the 1885 Gordon campaign just over a decade prior, and that there were only two of the correspondents, out of hundreds, that were still alive; he regretted they weren't all there to see the final death of Mahdism. Burleigh rode ahead of the main troops in order to relive and visit the sites of the 1885 campaign at Metemmeh, Abu Kru, Gubat and its environs, he also visited the old graves, such as that belonging to Cameron, the correspondent for The Standard whom he helped bury, the old forts and zerebas; and remembered the pain he felt upon receipt of the news of Gordon's death and his slaughter at Khartoum; During his explorations, he was shot at for his trouble. On 22nd August, he managed to reach camp before nightfall at Wady Hamed, located by the Sixth Cataract; as he rode in, he came across the Sirdar on an inspection trip who greeted him kindly and pointed him to the correspondents camp.

After his long ride in, it was imperative that he let his horses rest for a few days, so until his servants arrived with the back up horses and camping gear he travelled around on foot and slept on the bare earth, eating scrappy meals of biscuits and bully beef. After a few days of troop exercises, camp was broken and moved to within 40 miles of Omdurman. During this ride Burleigh managed another small detour to view the gorges of the 6th Cataract.

At the following camp the press correspondents developed a grievance; Burleigh drafted a letter which was signed by most of his fellow correspondents and sent it to Colonel Wingate, the press censor. The basis of the letter argued that The Times newspaper had two correspondents working for them, and although one officially represented the New York Herald, they got to wire twice the amount of words as the other correspondents at one time. This situation was reported to the Sirdar, who judged that The Times correspondents could only send 100 words each, although Colonel Rhodes (of Rhodesia fame), correspondent of The Times had pre-empted the judgement, stating that he would not use the wire at all.

THE CORRESPONDENTS, LEFT TO RIGHT, BENNET BURLEIGH, RENE BULL FRED VILLIERS AND HAMILTON WELLDON, IN THEIR CAMP SHORTLY BEFORE OMDURMAN.

    As the army camps got nearer to Omdurman, Burleigh was surprised that the Dervishes never harassed the army during the night; their swift feet and expert swordsmanship would have given them a great advantage, and Burleigh did not think that which could have occurred would have been pleasant at all. One morning, Burleigh climbed a small hill, and got his first glimpse of the dense lines of the enemies camp about 10 miles south at Kerreri. However, by the time they reached there on foot, the enemy had abandoned the place. A short distance south, another small hill was mounted by Burleigh called Surgham, from here he could see a distant Omdurman, the Mahdi's Tomb and Khartoum; however, between him and it, not three miles south, the whole of the Dervish army which he estimated to contain some 35,000 men lay in wait, they had left the city and were ready for battle. In the centre, he could clearly see the black flag of the Khalifa. Shortly afterwards Burleigh watched the British batteries as they started to bomb Omdurman, finding their range with the Mahdi's Tomb, which was destroyed by the third shot. The bombardment excited the Dervish and they were all set in motion against the British. Skirmishes started back and forth with the cavalry as they retired back to the British lines; the Sirdar was informed of the enemy coming en masse and by 3pm the British lines were ready. The Khalifa then took possession of the hill at Surgham; surveyed the British lines and decided not to attack that day; so it happened on the eve of the coming battle both armies rested quietly in their respective camps".

After this relatively peaceful night, just before four in the morning on September 2, 1898, the bugles woke the Sirdars 22,000 troops. At 5 am, after a breakfast of tea, coarse biscuits and tinned meat, the men were ready, which was just as well as it turned out that the now greatly reinforced army of the Khalifa, which Burleigh estimated to consist of some 50,000 men, was moving forward to attack; the British moved into their defensive positions.

Burleigh himself joined the Lancers for reconnaissance on Surgham hill and as he led his horse up the slopes, he "heard a mighty rumbling as of tempestuous rollers and surf bearing down upon a rock bound shore. When I had gone but a few strides farther there burst upon my sight a moving, undulating plain of men, flecked with banners and glistening steel. Who should count them? They were compact, not to be numbered. Their front from east to west extended over 3 miles, a dense mass flowing towards us. It was a great, deep bodied flood rather than an avalanche, advancing without flurry, solidly, with presage of power.

BURLEIGH EXAMINES A HOWITZER JUST PRIOR TO THE START OF THE BATTLE OF OMDURMAN.

The sound of their coming grew each instance louder, and became articulate. It was not alone the reverberation of the tread of horses and men's feet I heard and seemed to feel as well as hear, but a voiced continuous shouting and chanting - the Dervish invocation and battle challenge, 'Allah el Allah! Rasool Allah el Mahdi!' they reiterated in the vociferous rhymed rising measure, as they swept over the intervening ground. Their ranks were well kept, the serried lines marching with military regularity, with swaying of flags and brandishing of big bladed, cruel spears and two-edge swords. Emirs and chiefs on horseback rode in front and along the lines, gesticulating and marshalling their columns."

The battle of Omdurman began at 5.30am with a British salvo as the enemy streamed forward shouting Allah's name with confidence as it had long been prophesised that the infidel would be annihilated on this spot. The British guns had started firing from 2800 yards, smashing gaps in the Dervishes lines, but in no time at all, the range of fire had shifted to 1700 yards and then to less than a thousand yards. Then squadrons of the Lancers began firing into the tide of advancing men; horsemen left the Khalifa's lines in order to engage them, but they quickly fell back into the main body of troops. The Dervish columns hardly flinched at their slaughter, the men seemed indifferent to death, they hoped to charge the British lines, eventually though, they pushed for cover behind some western hills, and so ended the first phase of the action. Despite this mass slaughter of Dervish, Burleigh noted that this was so far the least dangerous battle the British had been involved in, suffering relatively few casualties. Minutes later, determined for a second attack, the Dervish dashed forward from shallow ravines, to within 900 yards, where the set up their standards and then were killed, Dervish after Dervish were shot down, riddled with bullets. "Then the dense columns shrank to companies, the companies to driblets, which finally fled westward to the hills." At 8am, the first action was virtually over and won; Burleigh thought the scene was more than human nature could bear, as he surveyed the10,000 corpses covering the landscape. In typical Dervish fashion some of the men were not dead and sniped away at the British from their resting places achieving some success.

During this campaign the Sirdar awarded the V.C. to a Colonel Smyth for saving the life of Burleigh and others. This extract from Burleighs account shows the active part (for a man in his late 50s) that he would take in battles / proceedings and also describes the actions of Smyth: "When the first phase of the action ceased at 8:30 a.m., hundreds, if not thousands of wounded Dervishes upon the field rose and moved away. Some of these were seen going back towards Omdurman, others walked towards the West to rejoin their friends. No attempt was made on our side to molest them, the order to "cease fire" having been given. It was either then or a little earlier that the large body of natives, possibly camp followers, behind the Khalifa's force, melted away, flowing back to the town. At that time some of our camp followers and servants, went forward from the zereba to pick up trophies from the field. A party of four went towards a small group of dead Dervishes lying about 300 yards on the left front of Maxwell's brigade. I noticed them picking up spears and swords. A correspondent rode out to join them, Mr. Bennet Stanford, who was formerly in the "Royals". In company with another colleague, I rode out from the British lines to join him, curious to see the effect of our fire. At that moment a Dervish arose, apparently unwounded, and spear in hand charged the servants, who incontinently bolted back to the zereba. My companion also turned back, but I was yet over 200 yards away, and so rode forward. One of the men attacked by the Dervish was a native non commissioned officer. He had followed the others out. Dropping upon his knee he aimed at the Dervish, but his Martini-Henry missed fire. He fired again and missed, then, the Dervish being very near him, ran for the zereba. Mr Bennett Stanford, who was splendidly, mounted, with a cocked four barrelled Lancaster pistol aimed deliberately at the Dervish, who turned towards him. Waiting till the jibbeh-clad warrior was but a score of paces or so off, Mr. Stanford fired, and appeared to miss also, for the Dervish without halt rushed at him, whereupon he easily avoided him, riding off. Then the Dervish turned to the soldier who, encumbered with his rifle, did not run swiftly. By that time I had drawn up so as to interpose between them, passing beyond the Dervish. I pulled up my rather sorry nag - my best was for carrying despatches - and took deliberate aim. The Dervish turned upon me as I wished. I fired and believe hit him, and as my horse was jibbing about, fired a second shot from my revolver with less success, then easily got out of the Dervishes reach. He had a heavy spear and showed no sign of throwing it is as I rode away, keeping well out of his reach. The camp followers by then were all safe, and so was the native soldier, Mr. Dervish having the field very much to himself. Thereupon an ADC, Lieutenant Smyth, came galloping out and riding hard past, fired at the fellow but missed. Checking his horse Lieutenant Smyth wheeled it about, and he and the Dervish collided. The man, who by this time appeared somewhat weak, grabbed the Lieutenant and strove to drive his lance into him. With great hardihood Lieutenant Smyth fired his revolver in the Dervishes face, killing him instantly. It was a wondrous narrow escape for the Lieutenant. The instant afterwards I asked him if he had been badly wounded, but he declared that he was untouched, a statement I could scarcely credit, and so repeated my question in another form, to receive a similar answer. In the excitement of the moment, he no doubt did not feel the slight spear wound he actually received upon the arm, which saved him from the thrust aimed at his body. An examination of the dead Dervish showed he had received four bullet wounds."

It had been assumed that the days fighting was now over, the fighting spirit having been knocked out of the Dervish, and that any they might come across would run away, but as the troops of the Sirdar left their zereba at 9am to march the six miles to Omdurman, they were being watched by thousands of eyes from the hills.

The 400 strong Lancers, who counted a young Winston Churchill in their number rode ahead of the main body of troops in order to make sure that the coast to Omdurman was clear and to clear out any stragglers. The riders entered one particular gully to take on what they thought was a handful of the enemy, but as they charged they realised that there were in fact several thousand men who had been hiding concealed and compact, ready for ambush, the Lancers were trapped, but managed to continue their instinctual charge without hesitation straight through this mass of bodies, Out the other end, both they and the Dervish had suffered many casualties, the Lancers dismounted and cleared out the enemy who remained, fighting their way out with their carbines. Burleigh wrote that during the charge, Churchill and another rode out to save two men who were trapped under their horses before the Dervishes could get them, but went on to add that it was debatable whether Churchill should have received his commendation, considering all the other unreported and unselfish acts that occurred during the battle. This, the last British cavalry charge of the 19th century brought up comparisons in the press with Britain's Charge of the Light Brigade at Balaklava, the heroic blunder of the Crimean War; However it did have its plus points in unnerving the enemy and is particularly remembered in that three Victoria Crosses were awarded to men involved in this action.

Throughout the final march to Omdurman, the undulating nature of the ground forced some of the British troops out of their relative positions, which Dervishes were swift to capitalise on as they "sprang from unsuspected lairs". On another occasion, some 20,000 Dervish dashed for the relatively small and isolated brigade of Colonel Macdonald which comprised some 3000 men. Nearly all of the British army could see from afar the danger that McDonald was in, and predicted the brigades annihilation. Burleigh himself remarked to a friend that Macdonald was in for a terrible time and wondered if any of his men would survive; Burleigh galloped to the top of the Surgham hill, regardless of any Dervish that may have been around, and witnessed the scene laid out below him. Help had been instantly sent to Macdonald but the closest brigade was a mile away, and the men were now beset on all sides. It was to become "a magnificent struggle", and Burleigh related the story of McDonald's courage, informing the public of his tough and protracted fight. Of the skirmish he wrote," neither in my experience, nor in my reading can I recall so strange and picturesque a series of incidents". He followed, "With a tact, coolness, and hardihood I have never seen equalled, Colonel Macdonald manoeuvred and fought with his men. They responded to his call with confidence and alacrity begotten of long acquaintance and implicit faith in their leader. He had led several of the battalions through a score of fierce fights and skirmishes, always emerging and covering himself and his men with glory, honour, and victory. All of them knew him; they were proud of him. Unmistakably, the Khalifa and his son, the Sheikh El Din, thought that their fortunate hour had come – that in detail they would destroy first MacDonald, then one by one the other Khedival brigades. What might have happened had both father and son arrived at the same time and distance on both sides of Macdonald, as was evidently intended, I will not venture to discuss. Happily the onslaught did not quite synchronise, and MacDonald was able to devote virtually his whole strength to the overthrow of the Khalifa's division before rapidly turning about first one, then another of his battalions to deal with the Sheikh El Din's unbroken columns ... steady as a gladiator, with what to some of us looked like inevitable disaster staring him in the face, Macdonald fought his brigade for all it was worth. The Dervishes came on in huge masses, waving their great flags and banners, Macdonald's brigade alone able to resist them. The enemy's cavalry were galloping for all they were worth into Macdonald's thin red line. The sight was fascinating, and it was impossible to unrivet one's eyes from the scene. The Sirdar stood on the hill with his glasses to his eyes. One could see the anxiety on his face. All this was bad enough, but there was still worse in store; a huge body of Dervishes, which had been hidden among the hills towards Kerreri were charging down upon Macdonald's right, and would cut off his retreat to the river. All hope seemed to be lost. Reinforcements were tearing up, but would never arrive in time. The boldest held their breath; the fate of Omdurman lay in the happenings of the next few seconds. Quicker than it takes to tell you, Macdonald broke his line in half and formed a right-angle, the cannons and Maxims were run back by hand, and the new onslaught was met by a deadly fire. He moved quickly upon the best possible ground, formed up, wheeled about, and stood to die or win. He was perfectly unaided. Indecision or flurry would have totally wrecked his brigade, and perhaps brought a further catastrophe to the British army".

For the first time in all his campaigns, Burleigh saw the Dervishes turn tail and run for the hills, McDonald and his men took all the honours of the fight, and he was dubbed "the hero of Omdurman". Upon the soldiers return to the British Isles, Burleigh, a good friend of "Fighting Mac" was often asked to address the crowds at clan and other functions held in Mac's honour, often electrify audiences, with his resounding, eloquent and passionate words.

By midday the army had reached the northern outskirts of Omdurman, Burleigh rode on ahead into the town as the main body of the army rested and took on food and water; he was sniped at by wounded Dervishes many times; some of whom surrendered to him and were directed to the British lines. He saw thousands of Dervish in the town, however several citizens came out and told them that the town would yield and that there would be no trouble, they also told him that the Khalifa was in his house and must surrender; surely enough, as the main body of British troops entered the town, the were greeted with welcoming cries by the women and children. Burleigh found the town to be a vile and dirty place, with no sanitary observances, and in the streets lay dead people and animals in all stages of purification.

That same evening Burleigh helped to release Charles Neufeld a European who had been held prisoner by the Khalifa for 12 years, prompting Neufeld to always refer to Burleigh as the "King of War Correspondents" . On his release, Neufeld was escorted to the army's mess when, " I heard a voice calling, 'Where's Neufeld?' and the inquirer introduced himself to me; it was Mr Bennet Burleigh, of the Daily Telegraph. I had heard, and yet had not heard, much English spoken to me, but the flood of language he poured out when he found me still in chains came as a revelation to me; it was as picturesque as his description of the battle which I have since read. Rushing off, he was back in a few moments with some farriers with their shoeing implements to try and remove my chains; off again, he came with some engineers, and amidst a running torrent of abuse, anent cold chisels and other implements which he required and which were not forthcoming, he questioned me". Burleigh was known for his expletives; a Captain Haig found Burleigh "a loathsome creature" with no manners. In 1896 he was thrown out of the tent of General Sir Rundle, who couldn't abide his foul language as he described his own capsizing on the Nile. Another story from a man named Cecil, describes a nice dinner he had with fellow soldiers which was mostly spent in abusing Burleighs attitude.

Burleigh was glad to leave Omdurman City for the British camps that night, where he wrote some brief despatches by candlelight and handed them to the censor, no doubt recalling as he lay to sleep fully clothed whilst trying to hold the rein of his horse the strange and picturesque events he had witnessed that day. In the confusion, his servants were missing, and there was no food or water to be had, and it was a full two days later when the servants and his baggage reappeared.

In Burleighs book, he recollects these times, the contents of which vary little from his accounts that were published in the Telegraph. He places emphasis on just how big a deal this victory was for both himself personally and the nation as a whole; that this battle was a bloody demonstration of the superiority of machine guns and artillery over older weapons. Nowadays given the British superiority and casualty figures, with some 10,000 Dervishes killed, 15,000 wounded and 5000 prisoners; compared to Kitchener's force losing 48 men with 382 wounded, the battle would seem to be more likened to a genocide than a fair fight. Burleigh commented, "The supreme and greatest victory ever achieved by British arms in the Sudan has been won by the Sirdar's ever-victorious forces, after one of the most picturesque battles of the century. At last, after fifteen vexatious years spent in trying to get here, an Anglo-Egyptian army has recovered Khartoum and occupied Omdurman. Gordon has been avenged and justified. The Dervishes have been overwhelmingly routed, Mahdism has been "smashed"". The Khalifa escaped from Omdurman and survived until 1899 - Kitchener was made an Earl, and given the title of Kitchener of Khartoum as a reflection of his victory.

There was one final thing for the British to do, and on 4th September, all the press were invited to go to Khartoum to attend the Gordon Memorial service, a sad ceremony which saw many of the men weeping. After the event the men explored the ruined Government house where they listened and speculated about the nature of Gordon's death. A few of the old campaigners shared a drop of champagne and discussed with the Sirdar the idea of a Memorial College in Khartoum in honour of Gordon. By one o'clock in the afternoon the men were back in Omdurman.

Burleigh's accounts of the battle of Omdurman and its aftermath also appeared in The Times. The Times had lost its two special correspondents: Frank Rhodes, elder brother of Cecil Rhodes, (the expansionist of South Africa, who Burleigh later met during the Boer War at his house "Groote Schuur", Cape Town.) was severely wounded in the right shoulder early in the day, and Hubert Howard, who had actually taken part in, and survived the cavalry charge, was later killed by friendly fire, just minutes after he had chatted with Burleigh about the adventures of the day as both men entered to explore the Khalifa's house. Without the news being covered by their own men for the rest of the campaign, it became a matter of urgency for The Times to make alternative arrangements. The manager of The Times, Moberly Bell, asked Winston Churchill, but he declined, and, in the meantime, they accepted the services of Burleigh by arrangement with the Daily Telegraph.

Immediately after the occupation of Khartoum, the Sirdar as good as ordered that all correspondents should leave the Sudan; and they all unanimously agreed, packing up their tents and selling their horses; Burleigh sold one horse for £1 - after he had paid £40 for it, and got little more for his others, though he fared better with the disposal of his camels and stores; the horses were pretty worthless in Sudan due to the country's limited grazing, so it was a case of accepting a knock down price or shooting them. Burleigh half wanted to stay to cover the Fashoda affair, but the Sirdar refused him both verbally and in writing; however, he felt a strong conviction that this story should be told to the British public as the issues involved were so tremendous that they could lead to a war between Britain and France. As the correspondents headed home, they travelled by "Messrs Cook's magnificent Nile steamer" to Cairo, stopping off at the Shepherds Hotel to rest up, before setting off on the final leg of their journey to England. After the men had crossed the Mediterranean, they caught the train for London at Brindisi, and as the train was pulling out of the station, Burleigh jumped off at the last minute, saying: "Goodbye, fellows; I'm going to stay behind"; his stunned colleagues had no time to inquire of his meaning but consoled themselves with the thought that their own despatches would reach London first. There was of course no "jolly old pals" about any group in which Burleigh formed a part; Burleigh had already passed his despatches and a map of the battle to a trusted messenger also on the train. This man was met at Calais by a member of staff of the Daily Telegraph who prepared the "copy" for the printers; the map was corrected by an officer who had been on the spot, and as soon as train arrived in London the copy was rushed into the hands of the compositors, and the map to the engraver's; the result of which meant that the whole story of Omdurman was in type before the official despatches of the Sirdar were in the hands of the Queen's printers.

Burleighs fellow train travelling correspondents did not know that Burleigh immediately meant to return to Cairo in order to cover the Fashoda affair; a Captain Marshand was rumoured to have been sent from the French Congo to Fashoda on the upper Nile in order that the French might open up their territories from their strongholds to the west, and hopefully find a route through to the upper Nile which they could then claim as their own, thus grasping the fruits of the British victory; another benefit to their plan was that it would cut off the British route down the Nile and through to Cape Town. The British censors would not let out a word of this over the wires, and although everybody engaged in the expedition was repeatedly warned not to disclose anything about it, several officers had kept a diary of the event which Burleigh used to relate the whole story on a day by day basis; Burleighs prior foresight in Brindisi was rewarded by the scoop of Captain Marshand flying the French flag in Fashoda. Such coups however made Burleigh unpopular amongst some of his fellow correspondents and his questioning of the soldiers who had been on the scene was much resented. A correspondent of Reuters said "I need hardly tell you that I have wired nothing about Fashoda except what I got from the British Agency - I cannot like Burleigh descend to interviewing Tommies in bars." The comment was perhaps one of envy.

Highly regarded as the most successful journalist of the Sudan campaigns, Burleighs work didn't go without criticism, he was accused of being too opinionated and bombastic. Soldiers themselves often claimed the press were biased to certain regiments; one of them was relieved to know that Burleighs account of the Atbara battle did not have too much of the "kilt" about it. One soldier charged Burleigh with approaching the Seaforths and asking for the name of its piper, as a gallant piper always tended to satisfy the British Public. Burleigh was also accused of making the battle of Atbara seem like a victory for white soldiers after he omitted to praise the two Sudanese divisions. Burleigh himself wasn't averse to a little plagiarism, describing the Omdurman rout with the words used to describe Britain's Crimean disaster, "Its is magnificent but it is not war".

    The Sudanese wars extended over 14 years causing the deaths of some 300,000 people, and allowed the flags of England and Egypt to fly unchallenged over the Nile. In 1898, Burleigh was able to say "Through half a score of battles or more, from the beginning to the death of Mahdism, I have followed British and Egyptian troops into action against the Dervishes. I knew General Hicks, but had the good fortune to miss accompanying his ill-fated expedition."
Burleigh also freely admitted that he had witnessed no better fighters in the world than the Dervish.

Chapter 4 - Madagascar 1894

Burleigh published another book in1896, called Two Campaigns, which covered the wars in Madagascar and Ashantee. The book itself is quite a rarity, and one of the few written in English that described Madagascar at the time, which owing to its unique natural history, was read as much for information about the war as it was for general interest in this "strange" land.

In the middle of December 1894, Burleigh set sail for the month long journey to Madagascar around the Cape of Good Hope. The French wanted Madagascar as a protectorate, and the two had been at war a little over a decade earlier and once again the French were determined to steal their prize and had practically declared war on the Malagasy.

The French had decided that no correspondents were to accompany their troops, so the Telegraph commissioned Burleigh " to write about the natives, their country, and the impending conflict"; consequently a lot of the book, unlike many of his others, goes into some quite interesting details regarding the lifestyles of the native inhabitants, as well as descriptions of the geography and flora and fauna of the island, and his own adventures.

Due to the prohibitions exercised by the French, who were particularly hostile to Burleigh, and went to great lengths to find him by searching random steam ships without a warrant on the chance they might apprehend him, Burleigh was forced to land his slow but comfortable and friendly ship some distance from the capital.

Nevertheless, upon arriving and landing at his first port, Fort Dauphin, Burleigh visited the Governor and was offered any assistance he might require. A short time later, he caught a ship with an American naturalist and traveller, Dr Abbot, which ran them a further 250 miles up the coast to Vatomandry, a little closer to the capital which is located in the heart of the island. Here the men spent some time exploring the local flora and fauna whilst enjoying the pleasant climate. They stayed under the roof of an Anglo American, which protected them from the night rains and the cool sea breeze of the day, but sleeping without mosquito nets meant they were continually pestered by small jumping black bugs which even copious amounts of eucalyptus oil failed to deter. Over the space of a few days they selected 38 porters to help them on the 150 mile march to the capital. Setting off late one afternoon they planned to march from dawn till dusk and cover on average 25 to 30 miles a day through the mountainous tracks and swamps, occasionally they were up to their necks wading through rivers. To help them on their journey, the Westerners had also enlisted the help of filanjana carriers, a local type of sedan chair. They men overnighted according to local custom in a provided native house wherein they could wash, sleep and eat in return for a small gratuity. The march was quite exhausting, the up hill down hill, narrow and slippery track was quite awful; but to ensure the success of the journey, the men had set themselves rules, breakfast at 4.30am consisted of chicken, eggs or sausages with biscuit or bread, and tea. They then marched until 10am when they had another more substantial spread, moving again until four or five o'clock, whence they rested in a village, and the best house they could find at that, they then bathed and had dinner, eventually snuggling down on the mat covered floor to sleep. Some nights the porters would make merry with a local rum, Burleigh commented - "How the rascals all snored after their guzzling and merry making! I often had to drive them to seek lodgings afar, at the other end of the village, so as to have a little sleep".

A few days into the trek he met his first European who was coming in the opposite direction, an Irish gold miner, for whom the war had destroyed his business. The group eventually reached the line of the forests, and for the next few days, they marched through pretty dells, bamboo groves and stately trees, encored with the screams of parrots and lemurs. After a few days of ascent through the cooler mountain passes Burleigh got his first glimpse of the seat of Madagascan authority and government, the capital, Antananarivo. Eventually arriving in "The Town of One Thousand" as the English translation describes it, on January 29th 1895, where he ended up staying in the house of Messrs Proctor Brothers of London, as the town had no cafés never mind hotels at that time.

On reaching the capital, Burleigh wrote to the islands Prime Minister, suggesting that there were two sides to every story, and that the case for the Malagasy had never been fully presented and he soon received a formal interview. In the interview, it was put to Burleigh that the treaty signed after the 1883-1885 war with the French did not submit Madagascar to a French protectorate nor would the people ever accept that, though they did want peace and were prepared to make other concessions for it. However, the negotiations had failed, and war was now imminent. The Malagasy had raised the red flag of war on the 12 sacred hills of Madagascar, which summoned everybody to help protect their land.

BURLEIGH ON THE MARCH IN MADAGASCAR.

Several days later, there was a mass meeting in a public space near the palace which was attended by over 50,000 largely untrained troops and civilians. The Queen arrived, carried in a velvet and gold palanquin, with a gold sceptre in her right hand and the crown resting near. She made a brave, defiant and rousing speech, the crowd cheered wildly, other leaders then spoke, and preparations for war were set underway. Before he had written a line about the event, Burleigh learnt that the French had been looking for him aboard ships; he was curious to learn why, and suspected that the French had banned journalists from Madagascar; it seemed the French had also barred all mail leaving and entering the country; but this rule was circumvented by the relatively successful use of private couriers who took the mail to British ships.

Shortly after his arrival in Antananarivo, Burleigh was through a friend, and to his great surprise, granted an interview with the Queen. This was a very rare occurrence, as the Queen usually declined to meet strangers and travellers to the court, and besides she seldom left her own four walls and hadn't even travelled over her own dominion. The interview took place in her palace and lasted two and a half hours. Burleigh of course started with a formal courtesy and a formal interview, presenting the Malagasy side of the story for the English speaking readers, (many of whom had previously took the word of the French and perhaps considered the Malagasy to be barbarians), once his notebook was shut however, things took a different turn, and Burleigh himself was quizzed about the art of warfare and the defence of Madagascar, he of course offered his opinions based on the experience of seeing wars in many lands, and suggested that the Western soldiers in the country be immediately involved and hired to train the local troops, and that ammunition should be made day and night as well as new weapons procured; he also suggested, that in order to hold the French off until the local troops were well trained, the Malagasy should consider offering mining rights to adventurers from South Africa after they had taken up arms to the Malagasy cause. Burleigh also stressed, that generally, a war would be futile, the French were well trained and the best that the Malagasy could do would be to hold them off and hope that political opinion in Europe changed; realistically though, it was stressed that if steps such as those he outlined were not undertaken immediately, the humane thing to do would be to surrender and come to terms.

BURLEIGH PICTURED IN ANTANANARIVO WITH THE INFLUENTIAL EUROPEANS AND MILITARY ADVISORS TO MADAGASCAR.

Burleigh soon became disappointed and quite angry with the inexperience of the Malagasy; little advice was heeded from the British officers who were brought to the Queens service such as the likes of Colonel St Leger Shrevington (pictured in front row - white suit and bow tie), nor were timely measures were taken to bolster the countries defences; this despite the French still being at sea. Burleigh felt the authorities did not understand the serious nature of the impending struggle, relying instead, as they always had done, on the slaying power of "Generals Forest and Fever"; (of the 15,000 French to land, 6000 were killed by the effects of the climate compared to just 20 in battle!)

Even a small build up and maintenance of the islands defences would have forced the French to send 50,000 rather than 15,000 troops. In a fine reflection of his life's experience, Burleigh wrote, "I have heard the battle-cries of many nationalities, in war and peace - Indian war "whoops", Confederate and Irish "yells", Saxon "hurrahs", Latin "hoo-hoos" and "huzzas", Arab "Allah el Allahs", but the Malagasy clicking shriek of the eagle was strangest of all. If they had been firmly and bravely led in action, and a fair chance at the French in forest or on the hillside had offered, I still believe that they would have "charged home"".

Eventually, come the middle of March 1895, the newly hired foreign military advisers felt that due to the inaction of the authorities they had no option but to resign. The Malagasy talked a good fight and would face death with sword and spear, but Burleigh cabled London and expressed his confident belief that all the French would have to do is walk straight into the capital as no resistance worth serious thought would oppose them. Burleigh did see some light at the end of the road, he thought that swift action by the French would destabilise the power of the nobles and that the general populous could then benefit from the building of roads and bridges across the country.

Despite the concerns of the Malagasy authorities for his personal safety, Burleigh decided to make a trip to the west in order to visit the forces engaged with the French landing force. The march was long, difficult and sparse, despite having numerous porters for his assistance, the floods of the season slowed them considerably. Clothes were generally wet and a trial to sleep in which added to Burleighs aches and pains, and although they passed through the plateaus that makeup the backbone of Madagascar, the altitude played little part in their hindrances. The scenery however was beautiful, sharp peaks, rounded heights, craters, lakes, streams and exotic plants numbed the pain somewhat, though he seemed to miss access to a good cup of tea! When he arrived at his destination there was no sure sign of a French advance, so he returned to the capital and decided to take a trip to the north as he had heard reports of several military disasters, and it appeared that the Malagasy defenders located there were little more than a mob, without stores, ammunition or discipline.

Burleigh was given permission by the local authorities to make the trip on the pretext that he wanted to visit some of the gold mines located there; he was accompanied by an Australian prospector, some native carriers and two Government messengers who he accused of being little more than spies on his movements. He felt he could perhaps discharge his duty by flanking the patriot army of the north-west, where he hoped at least to get a whisper of what was going on, even if fate was to mean that he could not become an eyewitness to the incidents of war. After several days hard journey, the men soon entered the tribal areas which were beyond the control of the ruling Hovas, a so called savage area where schools and the ringing of church bells had not yet reached. Burleigh felt that the majority of his party would have "bolted like deer" had they been attacked by a robber band en route - which they fully expected to occur, and though they did occasionally observe hungry brigands observing them, fate decided that they would be assaulted by neither man nor beast. The group eventually reached the town of Tsaratanana, which Burleigh found a distinct advantage, as the war news became ever the fresher and therefore more reliable. He quite enjoyed his stay, and found the heathen natives as much of a curiosity to him as he was to them. The trip also sent Burleigh towards the Northern hemisphere, and as he saw the "plough" his memory brought back sentiments of home. He generally walked in a dream of happiness, but his thoughts were tinged with a presentiment of death by his own fireside which unfortunately came true just several months after he wrote the words, and at an hour he feared most. This death, though not mentioned by name, refers to his second wife, Marion Sherer Burleigh who died in Wandsworth in June 1885. Burleigh later married for a third time to the Pole, Bertha Preuss in Wandsworth in September 1898 with whom he was to have a further family. The party decided to head on a little side trip to the gold areas which lay further north, though it seemed that the porters began to get nervous, and for two days refused to go further afield into robber country. They were eventually materially persuaded, and morally so after five indifferently armed soldiers were added to the company. It seemed Burleigh was the best armed of the lot, carrying a repeating rifle, two revolvers and a formidable Bowie knife presented to him previously in London by a member of the Peace Society. Burleigh started out on this journey with a bit of a cold, and given the harsh conditions of the trip he ended up contracting dengue fever, a virus that usually passes after a couple of weeks, but its symptoms for Burleigh included severe joint and muscle pain; in those days Dengue was known as break bone fever which perhaps gives a better idea of the pain he went through. Of course he used this disease to his advantage, insisting that they do not take the same route back to the capital, suggesting instead they should head west, this route would take them past some Malagasy military camps and possibly through the town Mevatanana, as well, which is where it all seemed to be going on, he adds "but that was a detail of no consequence, except to me". Just when he imagined that he had got his way, his porters again refused to budge, fearing the local tribes they might encounter; so instead of his plans coming to fruition, he instead made many side trips out of Tsaratanana. Before the group left to return to the capital, the presence of war had engendered a seething unrest and lawlessness in the country; so much so, that they returned back to the capital along the same path with an 16 extra soldiers in tow. One night the men set up a bivouac; Burleigh was not at all happy with the situation, but the porters again refused to move, so he went to sleep with his pistols and rifle close at hand believing that his defenders would disappear into the undergrowth at the first sign of trouble, and that it would be a case of every man for himself; and sure enough, that same evening as they were sleeping, some shots rang out and his guards bolted; Burleigh writes that a night attack is always a nervous affair, regardless of the fact that in this incident the assailants moved off as quick as they came; Burleigh moved his bivouac position just in case the raiders returned, though little sleep was to be had. The rest of the six week journey had little incident, and in hindsight he was glad to get out as the whole district was soon to relapse into outlawry. Some of the men who had attacked the camp, he was to find out, were later captured; the whole group numbered some thirty to forty spearmen who bolted when they heard the vigorous language of a white man, and presumed him to be well armed.

The rest of the campaign was reported from Antananarivo, though at first sight it still did not appear as if the country had been invaded. There were reports that came in, usually of a French victory here and there and of incitements to rebel in the capital, but Burleigh took all the rumours, good, bad and indifferent in his stride. As things heated up, some 40 British subjects held a meeting with missionaries, traders and miners all being present to discuss the immediate evacuation for women and children due to the possibility of riots, and where they might find the best strongly defensible building from which they could hold out against assault with their rifles. In the end, no resolution was forthcoming, and the general understanding was that it was every man for himself. As time wore on, sure signs of a Malagasy collapse became apparent; their troops were ineffective against the organisation and better weapons of the French. The French themselves took four months to reach the capital, a feat that should have taken 20 days, had they done so, they would have met little, if contemptible opposition. As the battles approached closer to the capital, Burleigh, who despaired of his not being allowed to follow the Malagasy troops, made an unauthorised rush to survey the capitals outer defences. However, it soon became apparent to him that positions almost impregnable to an enemy were being surrendered without a blow allowing the French to advance steadily on the capital. When the French reached the outskirts of the capital there was an exchange of shell fire, and when one of the shells burst in the Royal courtyard, causing the deaths of many men in front of the Queens own eyes, she instantly changed he mind, and to avoid a needless waste of life she ordered the surrender at 3.30pm September 30th 1895.

When the capital fell, the French cordoned off the area and immediately tried to locate Burleigh, inquiring where he could be found, as they intended to make an example of him. He couldn't understand their reasoning, though an official at the French War office said that they had no intention of shooting him, but intended to hang him! Naturally, Burleigh soon left for home and another mission, though in his book, he continues to consider the aftermath of the war and discuss some of the original local customs and the future of Madagascar. He also pondered, without conclusion, as to why the French war office would hate him, though he argues that they wouldn't have persuaded him to abandon his duty which he felt he undertook to the best of his ability.

Chapter 5 - The Ashantee Kingdom 1895-6

Having just returned from Madagascar, the old troubles between the British Government and Ashantee (now part of modern day Ghana) culminated; the British were still not impressed over some long standing grievances that had not been dealt with, such as the continued practice of slavery, human sacrifice, unpaid debts for previous disturbances with the British, and the neglect to open up roads for trade. King Prempeh of Coomassie was sent an ultimatum which he attempted to negotiate. Burleigh does concede that a lot of this conflict was also down to the fact that the British wanted to consolidate their territories West Africa, to prevent French land grabs. The date fixed for compliance to the ultimatum passed without response, so within a week, the war machine kicked into action. This Ashantee campaign was to yield "not even a whiff of gunpowder smoke," but it was to become notorious as the soldiers endured hardships far beyond those of ordinary warfare the malarial climate meant that the area that was already known as the white mans grave. On first appearances Burleigh couldn't quite understand the reputation that the area had for disease, but it was scourged with epidemics, and sometimes the mortality was rapid and terrible.

Burleigh procured himself a War Office licence, which entitled him to act as a correspondent, and to draw rations for himself and a servant beyond the frontier town of Prashu. There was a list of rules attached which was bound to obey, the most important being the appointment of a staff officer who would act as press censor, and through whom all correspondence was to pass; Burleigh was also forbidden to visit outposts without prior written permission and was not to use any cipher in his communications. However, on this trip, he was to break all his personal rules; undertaking long and tiring marches, sleeping outside, and taking no quinine, an anti malarial, but as luck had it, he suffered no ill effects, perhaps, thanks to his being recently seasoned in Madagascar; of the soldiers however, there were very few who escaped some sort of fever.

Burleigh left London for Liverpool via Euston station at midnight on Friday 29th November, 1895 in order to catch the boat; On arrival at Euston, he was greeted by some memorable scenes created by quite a crowd who were there to wish their loved ones goodbye. Of the departing soldiers he added, ""None but the brave deserve the fair", and judging from the numbers of pretty women at that railway station, they get them".

The train arrived in Liverpool at daybreak and the men were ready to board the S.S Loanda for a midday sail. Three days after leaving Liverpool, the weather cleared and overcoats became a burden; Burleigh passed a pleasant voyage by chatting on a daily basis with those who had lived and traded in their destination, learning a lot about the west Africa experience. En route a stop was made in Las Palmas, Grand Canary, and then they sailed on to Sierra Leone; in both places, fresh fruits were procured in order to offset the general effects of the "tinned commons". In Sierra Leone, Burleigh procured himself some porters and a cook, being told that these more northerly people were more trustworthy than those he might find further to the south, he also enjoyed some of the local cuisine which included eating some of the local pests - iguana and monkey! The ship soon weighed anchor and set off on the final leg to the Gold Coast. The nightly songs and dances were jollier than ever, being buoyed by the fine singing voices of the West Indian Regiment who had boarded at Sierra Leone.

On December 17th, the boat arrived off the pretty Arabic looking town of Cape Coast Castle, and two days later, the ship being considered the healthiest place for the men, scores of surf boats, handled by the local tribesmen, known as Fantees took the majority of passengers and crew to shore. Thousands more natives were on shore to help with the disembarkation of men, goods and stores. Within two hours, 300 men and 200 tons of freight were moved without a single hitch through the surf. Burleigh was one of the first off, and managed to find some temporary quarters in the "roof and four walls" Ebenezer Hotel at an extravagant rate, drinking water not included.

Burleigh got quite frustrated during this campaign as it was hindered by delays, which he knew cost lives. The rainy malarial season was due in February, and the soldiers were already dropping like flies. The delays and frustrations didn't stop the men having a Christmas knees up. The locals also got into the spirits of things, and despite their celebrations being more pagan in nature, they were joyous nonetheless; With Burleigh noting that it was, "not since I had been in Ireland had I heard such intense, perfervid fifing and drumming". All the talk around the Cape Coast Castle Christmas dinner table was that the natives would not fight but sue for peace, yet an hour later, the rumours had changed, stating that Baden Powell's scouts had had a brush with the enemy, and shots had been exchanged.

Burleigh left Cape Coast Castle and moved inland to Prashu on the 27th December, riding a light Wilkinson pneumatic bicycle which was terribly warm work as he was out of training and he found the bike barely capable of carrying his weight; he was also slightly lame, following a walking accident a few days previous. Of the experience, he noted: "The headquarters had left and I was in duty bound to catch up with them. Riding slowly through the rough streets of the town, I took the military road - the only one - for the Prashu. My fighting weight, with repeating Carbine, pistols and accessories - nice vague term - was 18 stone. Enough on a macadam, rather too much on an eight to fifteen feet wide, roughly graded, earthen and natural rock highway. Pedalling was necessary to move at quite a moderate speed, ' scorching' was out of the question - the sun had the monopoly of that, whilst as for ' coasting' downhill, an idling tree trunk lying across the road, a terraced ledge of rocks or other obstacle, played havoc with any race against time. I trundled on at eight to 10 miles an hour, contented with that speed and enveloped with a cloud of hot steam and dust. The swart natives who turned at the screech of my 'siren', and saw me on my 'bike', went white with fear, dropped their loads, and leaping the road scampered like deer into the bush. I saw them peeping after me as if I were a ghost or stalking fetish. There was a long downhill on a fairly good bit of road where, the path being tortuous, my 'bike' took charge before I was well aware of the fact. I had no brake, so 'coasting' furiously, shouting and pumping the siren till it roared, with my legs afloat in the air, I let 'her 'go. Those unhappy carriers, with whom the road was thronged, when they heard the uproar and saw me sailing down the wind on a cloud upon them, tossed their loads instantly aside, and they dived, scrambled and disappeared from sight in a twinkling. And down that half mile odd of hill their calls to their countrymen ran, as if I had bestrode a fire-engine careering madly through the streets of a city." In the end he managed to write off the bike, but ended up walking it back to the coast to take it home, where he engaged a blacksmith to repair it.

Burleigh, like most of the English population at this time, enjoyed his cycling. On June 20th 1891, the first "York Run" was held in England. The race was organised by the North Road Cycling Club, and the event required the 25 participants to ride from the General Post Office in London, starting at midnight, to the General Post Office in York within 21 hours 30 minutes, a distance of 200 miles (320 km). It is believed to be the first recorded occasion where an organised non-competitive ride of this nature took place. Post Offices were important for such endeavours as they possessed the only reliable clocks on display. Burleigh took an active interest in the event, though he described himself as a "stout, untrained, overworked man about town" who felt out of place among such champions; anyway he rode his "full roadster" as far as Highgate, when he had to turn to avoid another rider and a tram, which caused him to slip on the wet causeway, damaging his crank; he was not injured and persevered as far a Grantham (about half way) when thirst, hunger, fatigue and the damaged bike forced him onto a train so he could record the 10 leaders arrival in York at 9.30pm.

Back in Ashanti, Burleigh followed the troops from Prashu on their march to the highlands, located about half way on the road to Coomassie. The road to Prashu had been a busy affair, with people coming and going, but from here on in, barely a soul was to be seen. The road was very difficult, one night as he and some colleagues marched down a treacherous and foetid track, Burleigh fell several times, remarking that he was grateful that the Chaplain wasn't there "to hear my impromptu and hasty observations on things in general". A colleague of his became ill along the road and they had to wait in the dark until their exhausted porters turned up, who had taken three hours to cover the 5 or so miles; so it was decided to bivouac the night in the forest. The sick colleague had become quite delusional with his sickness, believing the savage carnivores of the forest such as the leopard were roaring nearby, Burleigh himself put the noises down to baboons, owls and amorous sloths. Luckily the night passed without the men being eaten, or plagued by mosquitoes and other biting insects. They woke early and carried on through the mist until they reached the next army halting station. As they advanced further towards Coomassie, Burleigh came across a group of traders who informed him that the King was making no preparations for war and that they believed no resistance would be offered. They traders agreed, that in reality the youth of the town were sick and tired of the human sacrifices that were made every time a notable died and were looking for change. However, it had been quite apparent to Burleigh since the start of January that bloodshed would be avoided.

Some of the troops took 20 days to cover the 150 miles to Coomassie; Burleigh claimed this was down to the baggage which was an even bigger burden on warfare than the newspaper correspondent! Illness and fatigue was put aside by the men as all were anxious to take part in the march to the capital. Marching at the front Burleigh was among the half a dozen European men who received a delegation from the King, a summary of this roadside meeting is as follows; "The King and his chiefs are ready to pay the indemnity, and he and his people will come under the white mans government". The natives wanted the treaty signed there and then to avoid the British entering the city, though the British insisted it would be done with the King in Coomassie. So the delegation left, and Burleigh was somewhat sore as they invited him to go to the capital with them, but military rules forbade him. Baden Powell, the leader of the advanced men then ordered him to return to the main body of troops that afternoon; which made him doubly sore as Baden Powell was not only an active officer, but drew extra pay working as a correspondent for a London paper. Burleigh grumbled a great deal with regard to this privileged competition, believing the officers were privy to inside information, and that it was in fact dangerous to try and do two jobs when life and limb were at stake. This was the first expedition in which the officer / correspondent role was allowed, many officers jumped at the chance to supplement their income because an officers salary was based on the assumption that he also had private means, many however did not. Burleigh argued that journalism was an official profession on a par with the Bar, and that he was there as a representative of the public, not the army or Government, citing the disclosures of their Crimean blunders barely 50 years before, and even his own disclosures regarding bending bayonets and jamming cartridges in the Sudan; the generals he believed, if left to their own devices would not write about such things and even mark down defeats as glorious victories. He may have been sore at the competition, but was later to be beyond speech, when Baden Powell scooped the fall of Coomassie just before the telegraph line was blown down!

The army were quite angry with Burleigh being a mile nearer Coomassie than he should have been; as punishment, they destroyed one of his telegrams and barred all movements by the correspondents; this order however was overturned but an hour later. The army did not want him to enter Coomassie before the troops. On the 16th January, with permission, Burleigh moved with his servants to within ten miles of the capital, spending the night under a rude shelter of boughs and banana leaves. A vicious storm broke that evening, leaving the men sat in puddles of water, soaked to the bone.

The following morning, the troops set off to the capital, Burleigh rushed ahead for nobody seemed to care that much, and got there well ahead of the troops. Here he beheld the King seated upon a chair, placed upon the topmost bank of a circular series of clay platforms; over his head were held huge plush umbrellas. Clamouring around the court were a hubbub of people, with an army of drummers and horn blowers keeping up a terrific din. It was the Kings favourite perch, here he would sit drinking, then throw his empty "death warrant" bottle at a passer-by who would be instantly despatched; with their bodies thrown into a nearby fetish grove, which Burleigh later described as being a stinking place, knee deep in skeletons. At 5pm, once the army were in place, the King was received, and told that the treaty would be signed the following day; Coomassie was won without a single shot being fired. All the soldiers were glad that the campaign hadn't become protracted, and that they would soon put the hardships and insidious climate behind them.

At 7.30am, the following morning, Monday 20th January, Governor Maxwell was ready to receive the Kings submission, but the King did not arrive, so two companies of the Special Service Corps were sent to fetch him from the Royal Palace with bayonets at the ready; Burleigh accompanied them. Upon arrival they were told the King was only just ready, as he had been waiting for some of his advisors, the British then pushed their way in nonetheless. It was 8.30 before the crowd were settled and the charges read out. The King submitted to the crown, and an offer of gold was made by the King, which fell well short of the British demands; and given the history of the Kings broken promises, the British arrested the King and other members of his family and made arrangements for them to be escorted to Cape Coast Castle. The palace was looted and some £2000 of sovereigns, gold dust and silver was procured, in order to pay towards the British expedition. Then a local fetish village, home to priests and sacrificial butchers was burnt to the ground, along with the sacrificial fetish groves; thus destroying the power that rested with the public celebration of charms and barbarous rites.

When the return march began, Burleigh accompanied the troops for some distance in case of ambush or an attempt to rescue the King. He soon turned back to Coomassie, to see what might happen after the British had left, only to find the Union Jack at half-mast, because the Queens son-in-law, Prince Henry, who had been a member of this expedition had died on the ship home due to fever. Burleigh had admired the Prince greatly, enjoying the visits he made to the press mess at Prashu for after dinner singing, story telling and merry making.

THE AUTHORS RETURN - MARCHING THROUGH A MILITARY CAMP IN ASHANTEE.

     Burleigh returned to Cape Coast Castle, walking unattended some 20-25 miles per day; on the road, he passed the British Headquarters, the captured King and many a celebratory native who seemed delighted with the Kings downfall. Another incident of this expedition that deserves mention, is that he stayed the night in a small village, only to discover the next morning, that less than a dozen yards away, "a wretched, tobacco smoking, drum whacking native guard", was sat atop 400lb's of explosives which had been connected to detonators by the British for use!. Come the middle of February, Burleigh was glad to be on the ship returning home.

Chapter 6 - The Great Boer War 1899-1902

The Boer War was contested between the British and the two independent Boer republics of the Orange Free State and the South African Republic (Transvaal Republic) from 11 October 1899 until 31 May 1902. Upon the conclusion of this long hard-fought war, the two independent republics were absorbed into the British Empire. Gold had been discovered in the Transvaal in 1886, which had led to thousands of British and other prospectors settling the land. The Boers, nervous and resentful denied the settlers voting rights and taxed the gold industry. President Kruger then gave manufacturing monopoly rights to a non-British operation, which infuriated the British, he also tried to build a railway bypassing the British ports, therefore avoiding British tariffs. Cecil Rhodes attempted a coup d'etat, this failed and war seemed inevitable. The failure to gain improved rights for Britons became a pretext to build up troops and manufacture a case for war, which the British thought would be quickly won. In September 1899, the Government sent an ultimatum demanding full equality for British citizens resident in Transvaal. Simultaneously, President Kruger, issued his own ultimatum giving the British 48 hours to withdraw all their troops from the border of Transvaal; otherwise the Transvaal, allied with the Orange Free State, would declare war. The Daily Telegraph, declared: 'of course there can only be one answer to this grotesque challenge. Kruger has asked for war and war he must have!'.

Writing from Ladysmith in October 1899, Burleigh, described how he had journeyed through the Boer army from Cape Town to the Transvaal; mingling with all those who had been called home to bear arms, he was quite amazed that they believed they would rout the British due to their superior marksmanship, though he considered that a month in the field would cure many of them of their fever. He stopped off at Pretoria to try to visit President Kruger, but the hour was inappropriate. The country seemed "consumed with the turmoil of coming war". Whilst in Pretoria, Burleigh invited himself to breakfast with his fierce rival, the correspondent Nevinson, and his companions - the Attorney General and State Secretary of the Free State; This action disgusted Nevinson and his friends, but they were too polite to say anything. Nevinson must have later regretted it, when he discovered Burleigh had sent off a telegram of his friends opinions in competition with the telegram sent by Nevinson!

Upon leaving Pretoria, Burleigh secured a free pass on the

commando train towards the Natal frontier which was transporting men, horses, fodder, stores and reserve ammunition. Nevinson claims it was he who secured the pass from the State Secretary, and Burleigh just tagged along. At around midnight, the train was involved in quite a violent collision, throwing the men and goods about, leaving Burleigh in a state of alarm and a cut upon his face. After 65 hours travelling (which in less fearless times would normally take closer to 20 hours), the train was stopped for the night as news came through that the British had been found planting dynamite to blow up the bridges.

Shortly afterwards, the Boer Commandant General Joubert, arrived on a train which had left Pretoria 15 hours later than Burleighs. Burleigh briefly chatted to the General and asked to be taken on his train the next day but no promise was made. At this point Nevinson, once again contradicts Burleighs version, by claiming it was he who secured passage with the General. Burleigh secured lodgings in the nearby town, but arrived back at the station early the next morning where he saw Joubert's train leaving. Burleigh audaciously persuaded the station master to stop the train and climbed aboard the Generals own saloon carriage. Nevinson says it was he who ordered the driver to stop, and whilst he did, Burleigh ordered a station hand to throw away all of Nevinsons' luggage, the loss of which greatly inconvenienced him during the campaign. Burleigh remarked of the event, "Evidently the sheer impudence of the thing must have shattered him, for he {Joubert} forgave me and came into the compartment, and we chatted for hours". Burleigh felt the General was a popular man amongst the Boers and through the clusters of men he got permission to take a photograph of the General and his more immediate friends.

In short, this conversation turned out to be one of Burleighs most important despatches of the campaign and gave him a great deal of fame. He reported that the General believed that the present and future were for the Boer, and that he would slit his own throat rather than give away one point of the Transvaal's claims, or if he doubted that God was on their side. The General had warmed to Burleigh so much that he secured him a truck that would take him to the almost deserted Natal border crossing at Charleston. It was from here that both correspondents sent long telegrams, Nevinson claiming that Burleigh went too far with his despatches by claiming to his paper, on the strength of a rumour, that the Boers crossed the British frontier every night; Nevinson claimed that this assertion helped to determine the start of the war, if indeed there was

A PHOTOGRAPH TAKEN BY BENNET BURLEIGH WHEN HE ALIGHTED THE BOER TRAIN OF GENERAL JOUBERT (WHITE BEARD, CENTRAL) WITH ASSOCIATES.

any hope of peace still remaining.

    Burleigh argued that the British Parliament had to either abdicate her power in the area or prepare for war, but the Governments leisurely diplomacy and aversion to invest money unless they were compelled to do so, led to many initial advantages and strategic positions going to the Boers. On his way to Ladysmith, Burleigh visited the town of Dundee to survey the area. At Dundee, on the 20th October, an isolated British column managed to overcome a Boer attack, causing their survivors to flee; during this skirmish, the power of the British Soldiers with their cannons and the excellent sharp shooting skills and cunning of the Boers were witnessed; causing Burleigh to comment that he liked to hold back a little more than usual, because at 900 yards the Boers shooting was passably good. The remaining Boers soon rallied, and their reinforcements forced the British column to steal away in the night and join the camp at Ladysmith.

    From his base in Ladysmith, Burleigh regularly rode out with the British troopers, and he was involved in many of their skirmishes, such as that at Elands Laagte, during which, the "target" of Burleighs horse and cart came in for a lot of attention from the Boer shells causing him to move them to the rear and continue on foot with the infantry to the top of a ridge. During the same battle, Melton Prior, the war artist, seemed to be attracting a lot of fire, and couldn't understand why, Burleigh came over, shouting, "Confound your white helmet, Prior; you are drawing all the fire!" Sure enough, upon the hats removal, the shot soon found a new objective. Learning his lesson Burleigh later covered his white horses and the white roof of his cart in permanganate of potash and water, thus giving them a ghostly neutral tint. The British were then ordered to advance, and the correspondents followed closely behind. Burleigh and Prior crawled to a wall by a tiny hut; an excellent position from which to watch the battle unfold, despite the bullets whizzing around "like hail". Prior crouched behind a wall, but Burleigh with his "devil may care manner", leant up against the wall, and watched the fight through his binoculars. Prior was sure he'd be hit. He survived, and at 6PM, the Boers started to retreat, and later that night Burleigh headed back to Ladysmith through the rain to send off his despatches.

Prior and Burleigh shared many exciting journeys together, the readers of the newspapers back home didn't realise that sometimes to get good stories, the journeys they undertook were hard and the roads dreadful. On one instance, Prior rolled out with Burleigh in his Cape Cart towards the Bloemfontein Waterworks, which were in the possession of the Boers, while the British troops were actively engaged in trying to take them. The enemy allowed the correspondents to go down to the building and then started shelling it. This occurred following a day's ride of 25 miles. On the other hand, the correspondents were English gentlemen to the end, riding out before breakfast in their pyjamas to the river to bathe.

November saw the start of a 4 month siege on Ladysmith. Burleigh had previously commented that the Ladysmith camp was a most indefensible position for a military camp, and had no strategic value, it had been bought years before only for its proximity to the town and water. It was overlooked and commanded by hills and mountains on all sides, and the town itself was visited day and night by nondescript visitors (Boer spies) who came and went at their own sweet will. It was thought that now the Boers were surrounding them in sufficient numbers, the British could come out and crush them and hopefully not see another within 20 miles of the town. The Boers from the hills and the British from the town fought a battle over broken country, covering a circuit some ten miles long; by the end of the afternoon, the casualties were light and about even; Burleigh however, thought that the strategic position of the Boers on the hills overlooking Ladysmith, and the forthcoming approach of General Joubert and the Free Staters from the north and west, meant that it was only a matter of hours before the whole of General White's British command and Ladysmith herself would be under siege.

Burleigh pleaded with his friend the war artist, "Prior my boy, it is all over; we are beaten, and it means investment. We shall be all locked up in Ladysmith". Consequently, Burleigh was one of the few correspondents to leave Ladysmith, and Churchill recalls how many of the correspondents laughed at his rush to leave, including his rival Nevinson who was happy to see him go after he had spent so much time debating the problem, and added that Frank Rhodes had compared him to the man who asks you whether he should marry a certain girl or not, and regardless of your opinion, will probably marry her anyway! However, even Nevinson agreed that he was probably right in going, which secured him a free run of the telegraph for his paper, whilst those who remained were soon invested and got very few messages out. So Burleigh left the comforts of the Royal Hotel in Ladysmith hoping that he would soon be able to re-establish communication with the representative he had left behind to chronicle the progress of the siege; he felt that the British had the necessary supplies to endure two months, but was disappointed that the non combatants of the town had not previously been asked to leave.

Writing from Pietermaritzburg on November 3rd 1899 Burleigh complained that things were now moving so fast that he was struggling to keep up with events despite writing with great haste; he had little time for rest and the writing of his own personal letters. He spent his days seeing to injured friends, interrogating Boer prisoners and trying to reopen communications with his man in Ladysmith. His life he said was not a happy one, his malaise was compounded by press censorship and the enforced delay of the press's messages for 22 hours, just in case the British public should find out something they perhaps shouldn't. It seemed to him that a correspondent was looked upon with suspicion, someone to be more guarded against than any Boer spy or sympathiser.

Writing from Estcourt, on November 13th 1899, which is located 30 miles due south of Ladysmith, Burleigh described how he used to climb the local hills from where he could hear the daily pounding of the cannon, and if the conditions were favourable, the sound of musketry around the Ladysmith area. Reinforcements of British troops slowly started amassing at Estcourt, as did the Boers, and on one ride out Burleigh saw parties of them within six miles of the city limits, and now that Estcourt was being threatened, the civilians left and those remaining slept with one eye open. Come November 17th, Burleigh wrote that a few exchanges of small arms fire had started to take place; however the event and talking point of the week, was the attack upon the armoured train which had left Estcourt to reconnoitre the Boer positions and was then derailed by a Boer ambush of shells on its return from Chieveley. Fierce fighting took place, leaving more than 100 British soldiers killed, wounded or captured, including Winston Churchill who was at the time the aristocratic correspondent for the Morning Post. This incident, Churchill's heroism, and his subsequent capture and escape made him a worldwide household name as his actions and gallantry were praised by many correspondents, including Burleigh.

During the Boer War, as we look at Bennet Burleigh, we are observing a man of nearly 60 years of age, he had been a correspondent for 20 years or so, a man with a lot of experience of life, death, war and its hardships, one could argue that he was at his peak, he himself was more than content to be a mere chronicler of the facts; In fact Burleigh's role encompassed so much more than just reporting the news to his fellow citizens back home, after his daily rides he would no doubt report back to those in command what, if anything, he had seen; but also, he only wanted the best for Tommy Aitkin's, and was quite happy, if not obliged to report the painful truths of what was really occurring out in the field; for instance, he complained that the War Office had failed to supply maps of Natal to the officers. He also claimed that the quality and quantity of Boer artillery had been overlooked, a surprise of the war was no doubt that the Boers possessed and knew how to use and position the newest and latest types of cannon and machine guns. The Boer guns seemed to have a longer range than those of the British, therefore he questioned whether the British powder was in fact inferior to the continental smokeless gunpowder. He did however find it fortunate that the Boer shells were not of a great quality, rarely exploding, and when they did, as they had generally plugged themselves into the ground they blew harmlessly upwards. He thought, though generalised, that the main problem with the conservative British Army was its lack of decision making when the troops took to the field, he felt this could be remedied, but thought that the lack of mobility in such circumstances was almost constitutional. He really believed that the only solution was to vastly increase the size of the mounted infantry and when on the march the vehicles for transport needed to be more numerous in order to supply the infantry better, enabling the men to force conclusions using sharp and decisive actions against the Boers.

A week or so later, around the vicinity of Estcourt, more small bodies of Boers were spotted, and it seemed that their intention was to move closer to the British troops. Two days later, the British had decided to stay and defend Estcourt, the location of which was far superior to that of Ladysmith. Two days after that, it seemed that Estcourt too had been surrounded, though it was never to be completely invested. In the ensuing Battle of Beacon Hill, Burleigh lost a close relative, from the Imperial Light Horse, who was pierced through the brain by a Boer bullet whilst helping the wounded. Burleigh went on to write about the operating room that had been set up in the local sanatorium where he noted that a Rontgen ray machine and an electric light would have been useful; "those who know anything of modern surgery are aware how useful the electric light can be made", something we quite take for granted these days. Despite these shortcomings, he had nothing but praise for the surgeons. Three days after they had surrounded the British at Estcourt, the Boers seemed to have the intention of retreating, and that they did, to Ladysmith.

On the 8th December, 1899, Burleigh wrote of General Bullers arrival at Frere, (the town to which the British army and Burleigh had moved after Estcourt.) signifying that the matter of the relief of Ladysmith was now at hand. Burleigh held General Buller in a high regard, feeling that once he was set loose, this stern and experienced leader and fighting soldier, would stand no nonsense and the Boer would finally be sent on the run.

Burleigh really wanted to send this report home, but the press were now being severely censored. The military argued that they did not want the Boers to find out about Bullers arrival, but Burleigh felt that the British Army system of press censorship was a sham and delusion; arguing that it was common knowledge amongst all the parties concerned - the Boers had spies all over. Burleigh felt that Buller owed this knowledge to the public, as did the correspondents - it was the public that they all served in the end.

Over a few days, the correspondents had been prevented from going to the front line; Burleigh found this situation ridiculous, as civilian onlookers and unauthorised pressmen were allowed through; there were no restrictions on foreign journalists. He also noted that the cable companies were developing a habit of breaking down on the eve of important events. Later in the war the correspondents were silenced again with the threat of the loss of their press licence.

In the meantime, the correspondents were annoyed at the embargoes, and decided to raise a formal protest which was presented to General Clery by Burleigh and an American journalist. The letter followed:

"Sir, - The licensed correspondents with this force respectfully desire to draw your attention to what they consider to be a great hardship to them, and to the interests they serve. On two occasions - one recently, and the other today, - we have been debarred from accompanying the troops, although in both instances there was a great likelihood that an action would ensue. The hardship is the greater in that while we were stopped … , {the} civilian visitors in camp, correspondents' cyclist servants, and others, have been permitted to accompany the troops afield. We ask that, as licensed correspondents, who are subject to an active censorship, and as gentlemen honestly seeking to do our duty, we be permitted to discharge those functions for which we have been commissioned. Very respectfully, your obedient servants, (signed by nearly all the correspondents)"

That same day, General Buller visited the correspondents camp and with a British attack on Ladysmith imminent, he unreservedly put his case regarding the correspondents plight to Burleigh; reminding him that they had undertaken not to proceed beyond the outposts without express permission, though he personally wished that they could see everything, and would not have been averse to them following the troops the previous day, though he did object to correspondents moving about freely at any time, wandering in and out from camp to camp. He also stated that he had no problem if a correspondent got the leader of a columns permission to join them, and then did so. Buller argued that what he wanted to avoid was a repetition of anything like the case of one correspondent who had gone outside and been captured, with the Boers refusing to regard him as a non belligerent, and asking for an exchange with an officer. The correspondents who had raised the initial protest, had all this explained to them, and accepted the explanation, empowering Burleigh to thank Sir Redvers Buller for his courtesy, which Burleigh did by letter.

BENNET BURLEIGH QUESTIONING THE RIGHTS
OF CORRESPONDENTS WITH GENERAL BULLER.

The British soon moved out of Frere in order to relieve Ladysmith, with the first main battle taking place in the Tugela region, which comprised a river, a bridge and an enemy embedded ridge. Once this position was taken, the British felt it would be "open going" to reach Ladysmith. The Boer entrenchment had been well prepared and neatly dug into the extensive range of bold and lofty ridges trending east and west. After two days of shelling, the Ladysmith relief column attacked the Boers with all arms. It was to be the biggest, most severe and inconclusive battle of the war. Of the engagement Burleigh favoured to report the truth as he felt this was the only way to impart a clearer knowledge, better efficiency and sterner resolution in the future. Of course during his reporting of the battle Burleigh wasn't averse to a bit of propaganda and jingoism; however, one must also remember that Burleigh only sent the telegrams, and much of his literary reputation owes a good deal to the Daily Telegraphs rewriter, a man named Arnold, who presented Burleighs copious and vivid messages as editorial.

The Boers unleashed a heavy fusillade of fire from within six hundred yards of the British infantry, with Burleigh proclaiming; "it seemed impossible that anything could face and live in that fire … Our indomitable soldiers walked erect and straight onwards. Not even Rome in her palmiest days ever possessed more devoted sons… the British soldiers, doomed to die, saluted, and then,… stepped forward to do their duty - glory or the grave"; he later added his view that smaller groups running from cover to cover would be far less wasteful of lives than the old habit of forming lines. Come the end of the days fierce fighting, which saw heavy losses, it appeared that no appreciable advance had been made in any direction, so a retirement was ordered. There were so many incidents that occurred in this battle that Burleigh was short of space to cover them all, and though this book is not the place for them, Burleigh went on to cover a lot more of them over several chapters in his book the "Natal Campaign" . Over Christmas 1899, a truce was observed at Chieveley, but not at Ladysmith, and sports and trials were the order of the day. On behalf of the Daily Telegraph, Burleigh took his Cape cart and called at the camps of each of the eight battalions, presenting cigars, cigarettes and cake to the men who were heartily thankful; Burleigh wished he could have done as much for those trapped in Ladysmith.

Passing no remarks in his book on the change to a new century, just the New Year, Burleigh and the correspondents moved back to Frere in order to be nearer General Bullers growing camp of reinforcements, and closer to the new press censor which Burleigh regarded as a thankless and uncongenial job; Burleigh was known to give them a hard time but only in the public interest of course. There had been six changes in two months within the office. He hoped that press censorship was not to become akin to losing his head.

In early January, it had been reported that Colenso was now to be watched rather than attacked and the rest of the force had to undertake a tough march west, towards Springfield. The Calvary went ahead and took possession of Swartz Kop, which was easily defensible and afforded a commanding position, with views of Spion Kop, Ladysmith and beyond. One day Burleigh rode to the top from where he could observe thousands of Boers at work digging trenches and building walls, drawing a line of defence in order to dispute the British right of way. Whilst on the summit, a heliograph (signalling apparatus that is used to send messages in Morse code by flashes of reflected sunlight) from Ladysmith was spotted trying to get the attention of Swartz Kop, they tried to get details of the British manoeuvres, but the details would not be given until the respondents learnt who the questioner was; it turned out to be a Captain Walker whom Burleigh new intimately, so he was the one who drafted the test message: "Who is Burleigh? Where did you see him last? Who represents the Daily Telegraph in Ladysmith?": the answer flashed back almost instantly, Only Walker could have known that they had met on the ship "Grantually Castle" on the way to Madagascar several years previously, and that Burleigh had sent a message to the Daily Telegraphs representative but two days previously via Weenen. The British soon commenced the bombardment of the Boer lines from Swartz Kop, alarming the enemy entrenched in the path of Spion Kop and Brakfontein; Burleigh, ever the Scot, described a Boer he saw being blown into the air by a 50lb shell, as flying like a Highlander would toss a caber.

(L-R) BURLEIGH, GENERAL HILDYARD AND MAJOR PRINCE CHRISTIAN VICTOR PICTURED ON THE EASTERN FRONT BY RENE BULL.

Writing from Potgieter's Drift at the Tugela river on January 22nd, 1900, Burleigh complained of being tired, the big country of Natal was pleasing to the eye, but riding back and forth each day across the long British front from the skirmishes and back to the telegraph was fatiguing to body and mind. The smaller skirmishes paled into insignificance, as all the correspondents wanted to catch the battle 8 to ten miles away being conducted by Sir Charles Warren as he attempted to turn the Boer's right. A few days previously, in order to see the demonstration against Brakfontein Burleigh himself crossed the Tugela river, but his voyage was a struggle, as he tried to keep his saddle-bags dry, his horse wandered aside and plunged them both into eight feet of water, destroying gear, books and equipment in the process. Man and beast swam for it, and got out together, wet and dirty, but not demoralised!

It was now three months since Ladysmith had been besieged, and the following week saw a lot of battles as the British slowly pushed forward towards the master key of the military situation, Spion Kop.

Burleigh took a tour around the vicinity of Spion Kop whilst the British were clearing the way to gain the summit during which he exchanged a few friendly observations and regrets with Sir Charles Warren, but generally all was going well. When the assault of Spion Kop finally came, things turned out to be a little different than expected, the British reached the summit easily enough, conquering it both secretly and at night, to within 150 yards of the furthest Boer trenches, but holding on to it was a different story. Burleigh left his observation post on the western base of Spion Kop at 6pm and all seemed quiet and well, though he did note the hundreds of casualties being ferried down the mountain, then things started to go wrong, Burleigh at first argued that a debatable order which should have seen the 60th withdraw and join up with the Scottish Rifles, was instead read as an order that the whole British force should retire, which left only a few soldiers on the summit. Burleighs opinion on this changed in February, when he discovered that some of the commanding officers had discussed retreat due to the terrible suffering that had been inflicted on the British troops throughout the day. The Boers then regained the evacuated position.

Come early February 1900, Burleigh wrote that although there was a general depression and humiliation around the fact that the British troops hadn't managed to pierce the Boer lines, he argued that the troops had never actually lost a battle, it was just that the Boers had held their ground. Burleigh neither defended nor sided with the actions of General Buller, admitting that it took courage to withdraw and live to fight another day, despite what the critics may say. By the fourth attempt Buller succeeded in breaking the lines and by February 27th the British managed to take the key Boer position at Pieter's Hill, and the next day, Lord Dundonald and his cavalry managed to enter Ladysmith relieving it after 119 days of an historic and memorable siege.

With "the intelligent anticipation of events", Burleigh predicted the relief of the town, and with the consent of the owners of the Daily Telegraph, packed his cart with tobacco, champagne, and tinned delicacies, sending it into the town to be welcomed with an outburst of joy. Burleigh had already joined up with Lord Roberts when he heard the gleeful news that the men who had been penned up in Ladysmith for 119 days had really appreciated his thoughtfulness. He then stayed with Roberts through the western campaign until the surrender of Pretoria when he was one of the first to enter the city.

FROM LEFT TO RIGHT, BENNET BURLEIGH, WINSTON CHURCHILL (AFTER HE ESCAPED CAPTURE) AND GENERAL FRENCH SHARING A JOKE ON THE ROAD TO PRETORIA.

Whilst in South Africa, Burleigh made the acquaintance of many interesting people; for instance:

He travelled from Pretoria to Waterval with Sir Arthur Conan Doyle in order to visit a recently liberated British prisoner of war camp. En route, the pair passed quite close to a Boer patrol, who were fortunately going about their own business and left them alone. On arrival at the camp, the men explored the several acre site, and went souvenir hunting, procuring amongst other things, a Boer Carbine, knitting needles made from barbed wire, and some leg fetters from the camp gaol.

Conan Doyle wasn't the only famous Victorian to get a ride in Burleighs cape cart. Twelve miles north of Bloemfontein on March 28th on their way to the battle of Karee Siding, Rudyard Kipling, who was staying at the same hotel as Burleigh, paid Burleigh the compliment of expressing a desire to accompany him to the field of battle. Kipling says that they went there in order to get closer to the English as they cleared some Boers out of a small woodland. Burleigh, perhaps temporarily influenced by calling to mind some of the works of the great writer and poet described events thus;

"To go voluntarily," he said, "where shells are bursting, scattering fire-hail of murderous missiles, and viperish bullets dart through the air, burn, and whip upon the ground, demands purpose and resolution. Mr. Kipling had both, and went forward. Fate and chance, with a little guiding, granted his desire ... We got to within 400 yards of the enemy, the bullets flew overhead, and we had to let the cart go, and escape amongst the kopjes. We were afoot upon a rather bare upland, without a stone any bigger than a marble, as Mr Kipling declared, and it truly was no place for two unarmed non-combatants. So we turned and walked south, towards where I had left the cart. At first the enemy were too busy with the cavalry to pay special attention to us, but with the horseman soon getting under cover, the enemy began to prove to us what excellent long-range shots they were when nobody was disturbing their aim by firing back. Still, we did not suffer, except that they hurt our feelings. Then they took to shelling us two poor wayfarers, and I altered my tactics by moving zigzag to the east, though once or twice they got near, all was well, and by and by we walked down the slope and so out of sight." The journey back was rather late, rough and bumpy; they arrived shaken but complete. Burleigh questioned whether Kipling would ever forgive him, he objected to having come under aimed fire. Though Burleigh added that he seemed to have enjoyed himself on the veldt, "making and humming over new verses, like Robert Burns was wont to do".

Kipling himself said of correspondents, that as well as good writers and observers, they needed "the power of glib speech…, the eye of a horse-coper, the skill of a cook, the constitution of a bullock, the digestion of an ostrich and an infinite adaptability to all circumstances." With regards to the written output of a war correspondent, some argued that "Burleigh could do it as well as Kipling, the only difference being that Kipling's price would be ten times the war correspondents".

Burleigh obviously impressed Kipling much, being used as the likely model for the senior correspondent, Torpenhow, in his novel "The Light that Failed". Kipling described Torpenhow as representing the Central Southern Syndicate, Burleigh first represented the Central News Agency; a man who knew every shift and change in postal arrangements, a man who could talk his way through a telegraph clerk when press regulations became burdensome. A man who could vividly paint a scene for the masses, and who knew that they preferred an insubordinate soldier disobeying his officers in order to save a fallen comrade. Torpenhow (the amalgamation of three names describing a hill from Yorkshire, Cumbria and Lancashire dialects) was a man used to being obeyed and took everything for granted. The novel is also interesting as it opens our eyes to the aspects of the war correspondents lives that were perhaps never noted elsewhere, in it, Kipling tells of a meeting between half the war correspondents of London at Torpenhow's house. In the scene he describes everybody talking at once, "discussing press censorships, railway routes, transport, water supply, the capacities of Generals - these in a language that would have horrified a trusting public - ranting, asserting, denouncing, and laughing at the top of their voices".

According to the war artist Mortimer Menpes, Burleigh was all of these things; " My first meeting with Mr. Bennett Burleigh was on the top of a kopje, when he handed me his card in the middle of a battle. He was the first correspondent I had met in South Africa, and he impressed me much. Mr. Burleigh suggests his name - a big, strong, keen fellow with a powerful voice, a man who looks in perfect health. He was the first to educate me in relation to battles. He seemed to have great habits, and to know everybody. He never hesitated to look through Lord Roberts telescope or to share a camp stool with General Pole-Carew."

Georgiana Spencer-Churchill Curzon Howe described him similarly, on leaving their rounds of a local hospital, both she and a Major Hale went to see Bennet Burleigh whose cape carts were drawn up in the market square, they spent the best part of an hour enjoying his conversation and hospitality. She said that he was Burleigh by name and burly in opinion and build, but proved an excellent companion, and interested her much with his reminisces of the campaign in the Natal.

Another man with an interesting tale with whom Burleigh was acquainted was the Australian, Breaker Morant. Jose Prendergast described how the men first met; "I was lunching one day at the Pretoria Club when Bennet Burleigh, the well-known war correspondent, told me that he had just lost the services of his despatch rider and asked me to recommend him a good daring rider and first-class bushman to take his place. All through life I have found that trifles often have serious consequences. I just happened, on my way to the club, to have seen crossing the square Morant ... I had not seen him for some considerable time. I bethought myself at once that Morant would be just the man to fit the billet. If I had not happened to see him I should certainly not have thought of him and Morant's career might have been a very different one. I told Burleigh that Morant was a gentleman, a good rider and bushman, and I didn't think he personally feared anything. Burleigh thanked me and offered to take him at once. Next morning Morant became his despatch rider". A similar story also comes from a Colonel Gordon of South Australia, who also claimed to be lunching at the Pretoria club with Burleigh, and that it was in fact he who recommended Morant as a gentleman, good rider, and bushman without fear.

Burleigh and Morant were remembered by Lieutenant Harbord in the Mount Nelson Hotel in Cape Town in November 1900; "Morant was one of the most amusing fellows I ever met, and a gifted raconteur. I remember one night at the Mount Nelson, when Bennet Burleigh and I sat up all night in his room, and I listened to those two telling stories. Laugh! I don't think I ever laughed so much in my life before or since, and it was broad daylight when we realised the time and cleared off to have a tub and breakfast." As the main war was now over, Burleigh was recalled by his paper, and Morant joined him on the trip to celebrate Christmas in England; his movements in England remain unknown, but he soon answered the call to return to South Africa as the war entered its final bloodthirsty guerrilla stage.

Due to Morant's literary accomplishments (he wrote ballads) and his excellent horsemanship, from where he got his nickname "Breaker". he was frequently "collared" by Burleigh as a dispatcher and assistant to cover operations away from the main body. It was one of these assignments that took Morant to the eastern Transvaal, and the eventual commission of Lieutenant in the Transvaal Constabulary. This was at a time when the period of enlistment for Australians was expiring, and Morant could have headed home.

As both the English and the Boers started to engage in a guerrilla type campaign, its is widely believed that Morant and his patrol had been incited by command to shoot their Boer prisoners. Morant is now widely regarded as the scapegoat of the Empire. The events led to a court-martial, after which Kitchener signed Morant's death warrant, in order to possibly appease the German Emperor for the death of a German missionary who had also been killed; it was hoped that this appeasement would allow the two warring sides to get around the peace table. The fervour around Morant's trial and death lasted most of the first decade of the century, he was executed in 1902, and ever the romantic poet, Morant's final words as he faced the firing squad - "Aim straight, you bastards!"

The author Kit Denton wrote a novel about Morant called "The Breaker", which he based on the historical records, Burleigh is mentioned alongside Morant in the work several times. The following extract, whether true or not, highlights Burleighs fame and is probably synonymous with many of his adventures and conversations. The Boers had ambushed the men during an evening's camp –

""My friend is no soldier, Let him go. He's only a civilian writer."
The Boer looked briefly at Burleigh. "A writer for the newspapers of London?" He accepted Burleigh's nod. "As bad as a soldier then. I have seen the lies that his sort has written about us." He saw Burleighs despatch case and in a swift move hooked it to him with his boot heel and kicked it into the fire. Burleighs involuntary move forward brought two rifle muzzles close to his chest and the Boer leader laughed without humour.
"If you don't like the treatment, scribbler, you should have stayed safe in England."

Harry had taken half a step forward, mouth open to object, but the leaders butt moved through a short, vicious arc into his ribs, doubling him over with the pain. Burleigh saw the mad flare of light in Harry's eyes. The Boer leader stood over the crouched man.
"You keep your English mouth shut, hear? We will eat and sleep a little before I decide what to do with you. And don't worry about being rescued, rednecks; your nearest friends are 7 miles away and my brothers patrol will have them by now. Turn around."

The two men were manhandled together, rifle-muzzles forcing them to move, and their hands were tied behind them. A rawhide rope was lashed two or three times round their chests, as they stood back-to-back, and then the leaders hands on their shoulders crammed them down to the ground, sitting awkwardly, knees high, away from the fire. Two of the Boers were systematically going through their saddle bags, pulling out the little food they had left, taking the clothes, tossing other things aside. The prisoners watched as the Boers began to prepare food. Burleigh, his head craning back and half-turned, whispered, "What do you suppose they'll do, Harry?" He tried to keep his voice calm, but Harry heard the slight tremble in it and thought, no point in not telling him the truth.

"Knife us, I should think, Ben. Makes no noise ... and saves bullets."

Burleighs back tensed against his, then relaxed. "That bloody Boer was right, wasn't he? I should have stayed at home!" ...

BURLEIGH FAR RIGHT WITH MORANT FAR LEFT.

The British public loved Burleighs writings, and although he was first and foremost a war correspondent, he was also linked to the British Intelligence Department. It is written that he had an incredible knack of picking up information within the town, such as the workings of the local gold mines after they were confiscated by the Boers, as well as many an amusing tale of some of the hoarding propensities of some of the Boer leaders under Kruger as tales of buried riches in the Johannesburg area became rife.

Burleighs extra curricular activities didn't stop at intelligence gathering; he was a formidable enemy of his opponents, such as Colonel

Blake of the Boers, who wrote of a scathing hatred for Burleigh in his memoirs: When the British occupied Johannesburg, they heard that Colonel Blake was still in the city, and they wanted him badly, so much so that the man fortunate enough to capture him was in line for a neat sum of money. Blake said of Burleigh, he "was not a combatant.; he was a war correspondent, and not supposed to take any active part". Late one night, the proprietor of the American Hotel was aroused and on opening the door, he was faced with Bennet Burleigh carrying a revolver. In the next room, he proceeded to aim the revolver at a sleeping mans head and said, "I have you at last, Blake, and you are good meat"; however it was the wrong man; this did not stop Burleigh and a few nights later he returned only to find the wrong man again, and Blake goes on to say that this "non combatant, was sorely disappointed. Had this thing, Bennet Burleigh, been captured by the Boers, he would have whined and cried and begged to be released". Adding that "Bennet Burleigh is a cowardly thing, and such a thing cannot possibly make a truthful report. Take all his writings during the war, and I very much doubt whether one grain of truth could be found in any one of his reports. We read many of his detailed descriptions, and they were so ridiculously false that we could not help laughing. Mr Bennet Burleigh, you are a thorough-bred Englishman, typical of a degenerate race, and I now drop you as I pick you up, a dirty thing".

An Englishman, Major Gardner, who was also present in South Africa, also disliked Burleigh, he felt he exaggerated his own importance and assumed a dictatorial attitude towards the military authorities; however, he also gave him his dues, describing him as unquestionably enterprising and brave. Another man who criticised Burleighs role in the Boer War was the correspondent H.W. Nevinson. The pairs rivalry was highlighted previously on the train ride with General Joubert. Nevinson recalled in his memoirs the boat trip over to South Africa, where he described Burleigh as dominating the ship with "his strident voice and a boisterous manner of apparent bonhomie"; he claims Burleigh lost some of his reputation during this war partly for his insistence on giving good advice to Generals and his "smartness" towards other correspondents; this attitude left him an object of pity as he sat isolated ,shunned and forgotten during later campaigns, displaying more imagination than accuracy in his descriptions of the battles between the Turks and Bulgars.

When it appeared the war was coming to an end and that the British would be victorious, Mr Amery, the head of the correspondents working for The Times, who later became a prominent British politician witnessed the surrender of General Cronje on the 27th February near Jacobsdal. That evening he went to check into a hotel, but it was full; he was told he could join the many others and sleep on the dining room floor. "In trying to do so in the dark I fell over a large, soft mass which proceeded to give vent to its feelings in a voice and language which I at once recognised as belonging to old Bennet Burleigh, who had, apparently, just come round from Natal, thus missing both the imminent relief of Ladysmith and Cronje's surrender. I couldn't help condoling with him, but he just chuckled: "That's all you know about it, my boy." He was right, for despite Burleigh having followed Sir Redvers Buller's campaign, the Daily Telegraph's account of Cronje's surrender was as complete, and as full of little touches suggesting an eyewitnesses story, as any of the others". Burleigh was very adept at getting stories and information from people - towards the end of March 1900, during which Burleigh had joined Lord Roberts's offensive against Bloemfontein, Burleigh sat down to breakfast with a Colonel Leachman, who would later remark in his diary that thanks to their chat there would "be a lot of trumpeting in the Daily Telegraph about the actions and harassments of a column of men during the very long march to Bloemfontein".

BURLEIGH WITH PEARCE
OF THE DAILY NEWS

The correspondents also made the news themselves. Upon the surrender of Bloemfontein, the correspondents who were with Lord Roberts when the Boers left, raced on horseback to the city. The picture, which currently hangs in the foyer of the Daily Telegraph, shows Burleigh, on the 14th April 1900, returning to Lord Roberts bringing the news that Bloemfontein had indeed surrendered. This story appeared in the illustrated newspaper Black and White, which Burleigh had joined in 1900, he did a lot of freelance work for other papers such as this and the Scottish Leader. He was also employed for quite a number of years by a press association in New York, to whom he cabled letters for distribution to newspapers in the United States. There is also a contradiction to this story, a certain Mr Morrison claims that in fact he was the first to inform Lord Roberts of Bloemfontein's surrender, however, he argues that he was well used to correspondents staying out of harms way during battles, only to blaze forth to the front in their prose. He despised the sickening mutual admiration of the correspondents that compelled Melton Prior to draw Burleigh undertaking this historic action, rather than himself.

BURLEIGH INFORMS LORD ROBERTS THAT BLOEMFONTAIN HAS SURRENDERED.

    During the final negotiations for peace in Pretoria, Lord Kitchener gave orders that no hint of them should be despatched, but once Burleigh was sure that they were succeeding, his reputation for moroseness served his paper well. Burleigh was never known to go out of his way to express goodwill to anybody or to bother unduly about his family. So when, on Whit Monday 1902, the owner of the Telegraph, Edward Lawson received a strangely polite message from the dour Scotsman which read "Whitsuntide greetings", and at the same time Burleigh's brother got a message "returning tell Lawson" it became obvious to The Telegraph that something was up; Burleigh was not the kind of man to abandon his post without instruction.

He had sent two very innocent messages that no censor would dream of stopping. However, the cables were dated Whit Monday, and when the owner of the Telegraph read the gospel of the day "peace I leave with you, my peace I give unto you", it clicked and the next morning, the Telegraph came out with the news that terms had been agreed and a few days later the peace was signed. The following account of events was printed in the Daily Telegraph:

" On Whit Monday, Mr Burleigh telegraphed us from Pretoria the following message: 'Whitsuntide greetings!' When his despatch reached us without any official delay our first idea was that its transmission at full rate from the seat of war was a somewhat superfluous demonstration of politeness. A little reflection, however, served to indicate the significance of the particular season at which the sociable sentiment was expressed; and we fortunately remembered that in the Eastern churches the symbol of Whitsuntide was the dove of Peace. But on this surmise we did not feel justified in making any comment. We turned, however to the Prayer Book - knowing Mr Burleigh to be well acquainted with holy writ - and, reading over the Gospel for Whitsunday, we came upon the following sentence:
' Peace I leave with you; my peace and I give unto you; not as the world giveth, give I unto you. Let not your heart be troubled, neither let it be afraid.'
Even then we did not feel justified in coming to a fixed conclusion. But when we received Mr Burleighs message to his brother in Glasgow- 'Returning. Tell Lawson' - we felt that the moment had arrived when we might fairly take the public into our confidence."

However, despite evidence to the contrary, Burleighs involvement with the Boers wasn't all so egocentric. After the war, Burleigh acted as an auctioneer for a fund to help the Boer orphans and widows. The Boer authoress of the event, described him as that "same fat war-correspondent Bennet Burleigh", who she had earlier praised for teaching her to make mint julep (a drink based on Bourbon). Burleigh took the responsibility to sell various sketches and pictures, the bidding was brisk, particularly from one man, who all but ceased bidding when Burleigh called out during the sale of a slower item, "Come on, Mr Millionaire!". The diary of the 9th Lancers, states that the "lightning sketches" made by the war artists Melton Prior and Woollen made the following prices, Lord Roberts, by Prior - 75 guineas, Kruger, by Woollen, 33 guineas; these and other pictures sold for a grand total of 134 guineas.

In a letter to Winston Churchill from General Buller, congratulating both him and Oldham on his success of being elected an M.P., dated November 1900, Buller mentions that he travelled back to England on the same ship as Burleigh, adding that "he is I think played out". Perhaps, it seems the Boer war had taken its toll on this now 60 year old man, it seems he was, by now, generally disillusioned and disheartened; the attitude of the military and its censors towards the correspondents had changed.

Finally, with regard to Burleighs book about the war, "The Natal Campaign", The New York times reported in August, 1902, that the much advertised Burleigh was to release the longest and most elaborate book on the South African war to date, and that the publishers were hotly competing for it. For his role in the war, Burleigh and several other correspondents were awarded the Queens South Africa Medal on 18th March 1903. To receive this war medal, the correspondent had to have been accredited by the editor of the newspaper he represented, reported by telegraph and not by letter, and to have held a pass from the Chief Censor and also to have served with the troops in the field.

BURLEIGH SPORTING HIS QUEENS SOUTH AFRICA MEDAL

Chapter 7 - Russia / Japan War 1904-1905.

This war featuring the colossus of Russia against upstart Japan aroused a great deal of international interest. The Americans were interested as they saw the territorial and racial differences affecting their own interests, and the British, though not involved, because the Russians had been encroaching on their own borders in India.

BURLEIGH WITH BARON IWASAKI IN MANCHURIA

The above picture was of great interest at the time, as the telegrams and letters of Burleigh were read widely in the English speaking world; until then, the general populace had a very limited knowledge of the Far East. This photograph was taken in Mukden and Burleighs wife produced this sketch from it. It shows Burleigh with a Scottish gentleman, Mr Glover, and Baron Iwasaki, the head of Mitsubishi, and Japans wealthiest man, with whom Burleigh had travelled to the Far East.

In October 1903 Burleigh had the following conversation with his chief and deputy in Fleet Street; "What do you think of the state of affairs in the Balkans?", they enquired, adding "There is sure to be war! So hadn't you better be off, and on the spot?"; Burleigh disagreed, "No; I don't believe anything serious will take place there at present. There are at least two powers too deeply interested that will insist on preserving the peace. Other correspondents have gone thither, I know, but they will only have had a journey, and no more."

"Well, then, what about the Far East?"

"Ah yes, the increasing friction between Russia and Japan is quite another affair. Conflict may occur there any day, for there appears no way out of the position but surrender by one or the other, or war."

Covering this campaign for the Glasgow Herald and Daily Telegraph, Burleigh set off two days later, and having little faith in the Trans-Siberian express, he started out from Liverpool on the Cunard liner Luciana to America. He arrived at Ellis Island, New York on October 24th 1903. The immigration records give his age as 56, a mistake perhaps, or perhaps done purposefully in order to make it appear that he would only be 18 at the end of the American Civil War, thus deflecting any suspicions.

Upon his arrival in New York, Burleigh was none to pleased at the changes that had been made since he left, a green and verdant land was now dwarfed under the horrid shadows of rising steel and masonry; he knew the Americans were sensitive to criticism, but felt he had the right as both his grandfathers were buried on its shores, and because he was "further bound thereunto by other ties and disservices".

On his way to Japan Burleigh had to travel across the USA, and on the way through he called in with the Wright Brothers who had made their first glider flight in 1900, their archive collection holds Burleighs business card; to which he had added his home address on the back. The Wrights later developed a powered machine, which just months after Burleighs visit, on December 17th 1903, flew at Kitty Hawk, North Carolina. The flight wasn't much -12 seconds and 120 feet, but it was the first controlled, sustained flight in a heavier-than-air craft, and one of the great moments of the century. The brothers flew 3 more times that day, covering more distance as they got used to the way the large front rudder responded in flight. Orville's second flight was 200 feet, and Wilbur's before it nearly as long. But the final flight of the day carried Wilbur 852 feet in 59 seconds. Burleigh witnessed some of the hubbub in the run up to Kitty Hawk, and wrote about it in the Telegraph, only to find that the general public of Europe regarded the articles as sensationalism and were not prepared to welcome the conquest of the air. It seems they thought that air travel would never take off. (One of Burleighs jokes - not mine!)

Bennet Burleigh,

Daily Telegraph, London.

4 Victoria Road
Clapham Common
London S.W.

COPY OF BURLEIGHS BUSINESS CARD PRESENTED TO THE WRIGHT BROTHERS.

After his visit, Burleigh continued by train across what was now a tamed country to the pacific seaboard and Vancouver. Here he boarded the liner "Empress of Japan"; en route, a sailor was lost overboard, and his Japanese millionaire friend Baron Iwasaki suggested they make a collection for his dependants. They sailed on past the Aleutian Islands eventually dropping anchor at Yokohama. Thanks to the power and kindness of Baron Iwasaki, it seems Burleigh was swiftly helped ashore and taken through customs, finding himself lodged at the Imperial Hotel, Tokyo, within two hours. From my personal collection, I have a letter written by Burleigh on the hotels stationary to his boss Sir Edwin Arnold, thanking him for his letter of introduction to H.E. Marquis Ito, one of Japans most prominent men, and a major driving force behind countries

Westernisation. A powerful man who Burleigh much admired and

Leading Hotel of the Far East
Imperial Hotel, Ltd., Tokio.
Emil Flaig.   Manager.

Tokyo, 2ⁿᵈ January 1904

My dear Sir Edwin,

    I thank you for the letter of introduction to H.E. Marquis Ito, which I delivered through his kindness into his own hands. Your letters, nor indeed any others from home, did not reach me until Xmas day. I have no doubt but that I will be placed in a position, thanks to your influence, where I can see the fighting that now seems very certain, and very near. Had I not been so hurried in leaving London, — two days — I would have called upon you but I trust to have that honor and pleasure when I get back. Meanwhile accept my profound thanks for your too flattering letters

Yours very Sincerely & Respectfully,
Bennet Burleigh

LETTER FROM AUTHORS PRIVATE COLLECTION.

interviewed several times.

In the first few chapters of his book, "Empire of the East, or Japan and Russia at war 1904-5" Burleigh describes the Japanese military system, and provides the evidence that this patriotic people were gearing up for war; he then spends sometime describing, in a quite favourable light, the society, history and customs of Japan, depicting scenes and details as interesting to the modern reader as they were back in the day. Unfortunately, due to the fact that Burleigh was made a virtual prisoner of the Japanese military, he couldn't get to the front to witness the events of war, so most of this book is a description of events and battles from afar, leaving us little evidence to know more about Burleigh the man. After a while, it seemed that the negotiations between the warring parties were going to become quite prolonged, and feeling the need for a bit of adventure, he decided to leave Tokyo to see what was happening elsewhere. He took the train south to Nagasaki, a tiresome and uncomfortable journey for such a big man in a world he felt was designed for much smaller people.

At Nagasaki Burleigh waited on the Russian steamer, Argun, which was to head through the Yellow Sea to what is now known as Dalian, located on the Liaodong Peninsula, China, but was then called Dalny, Manchuria; this town connected up with the Trans-Siberian railway and was a town that the Russians hoped to build into a city as it was ideally located on a peninsula that the Russians wanted to fortify and absorb in order to increase and control trade with the east. After disembarkation, he first came across Russian bureaucracy in trying to get his passport cleared, and ended up having to reside in a grotty hotel basement room. After surveying the Russians defences he soon moved inland to Mukden, the ancient capital of Manchuria; here he hired a rickshaw for a five mile tour of the ancient three walled town.

As he travelled through Manchuria, he noticed many a Japanese spy disguised as a Chinaman. As Christmas was coming, he joined the local Christian missions for mass; after observing the Russian supply line and garrison preparations, he soon headed back to the port, where he decided to sleep on a ships deck rather than in the hotel whilst waiting for the Japanese to decide when they would begin to shoot.

In the meantime, the Japanese were turning the screw on press freedoms, numerous rules and regulations were given out, purely with the intention of causing endless annoyances both petty and great; so much so that Burleigh was sure, if many of the pressmen knew what was to come, they would have gladly left for home sooner rather than later. For instance, feeling the war would be a naval one Burleigh tried to get passage on a Japanese ship, but to no avail, the authorities were determined to be in control and press passes were not to be issued until war was declared. The Japanese press were to be allowed to go with the navy, but the foreigners were only permitted to follow the army.

Eventually, the diplomatic route failed to open any ground and the Japanese began hostilities on the evening of February 8h at Port Arthur. Whilst the Russian crews idled, drank and enjoyed themselves ashore, at around midnight out of nowhere appeared three or four Japanese torpedo boats which proceeded to pummel the Russian battleships. Early resistance was feeble, but the Russians soon woke up, and the land batteries forced the Japanese to withdraw, having destroyed 5 or 6 Russian men-o'-war. The Japanese returned an hour later, and launched a second equally successful attack before escaping. Later that day the Japanese returned with a stronger force, and started bombarding the port once again. Meanwhile, at Chemulpo port, Korea; the Japanese fleet was met by two Russian ships; and, heavily outnumbering the Russians, the Japanese were again victorious. Simultaneously, in mainland Manchuria, the Japanese forces began to blow up Russian railway bridges and cut telegraph wires.

Once the Japanese were happy that they had blockaded Port Arthur, and therefore had control of the seas, the second phase of the war began. Burleigh discussed the unhindered transport of the Japanese troops, and the likelihood that these men would take the Liaodong peninsula with ease. He then predicted that the Japanese would and could, given time, take Port Arthur by investment rather than assault.

Burleigh soon found himself taking a steamer across to the western side of Korea, landing near Seoul, in order to join the Japanese land preparations. Burleigh, started this campaign on a pony " somewhat bigger than a St Bernard dog, and neither so sturdy as an Egyptian donkey." However being a large man, he soon realised that he was going to have to walk the fields of battle; despite his thoughts of being pursued by an angry Cossack. At this time of year, the water in the ports of Northern Korea was still frozen, so the troops had to endure long and cold marches up to the borderlands of Manchuria and Korea, here, the Japanese amassed three armies, in order to protect their rear and flank, up and down the natural frontier that was the Yalu river. As the Japanese and Russians started to skirmish on land, the Japanese slowly began to show their superiority, eventually obtaining a foothold in Manchuria.

Early in April, the ice started to break up, and thus increased the floes on the Yalu river making further Japanese incursions into Manchuria impossible, so Burleigh headed back to Tokyo for a short time. By the second week of May, those correspondents and attaches that had been permitted to go to the front were allowed to leave Tokyo and join the Second Army. Burleigh though was not best pleased, as his friend, the war artist, Melton Prior who had been stuck in Tokyo himself as a virtual prisoner for three months explained on May 5th; " I cannot help myself when we realise that Bennet Burleigh, the most experienced and interesting correspondent of the day, has had to come here, and wait events. He arrived about two weeks ago from Korea and he left his servants and horses, provisions, tent, etc, at Chemulpo, and now he is told by the heads of the War Department that he must bring them all here if he intends going with the second column".

However, there were many more frustrating delays; the Japanese were very stubborn, and on May 30th, Prior wrote that the pressmen had sent a very strong letter, written by Burleigh, in order to try to get the ministers to influence the authorities to allow them to go to the front. The chief American correspondent and Bennet Burleigh visited Japanese General Fukushima, and explained that they should be allowed to go to the front. They explained that they did not want anything from the army, and that they would look after themselves, but the general replied that the press with the first column had caused so much trouble and complained so much that he did not know what to do.

Finally, after months of fretful waiting, on the 19th of July, there came word that they were going to the front to see the fight for Port Arthur. On July 24th Burleigh was very busy carrying his luggage, paying wages, making arrangements with banks, and the numerous other tasks of a war correspondent. As the boat got to within the sound of the cannon battles for Port Arthur, they were forced to turn their backs on this scene, as they were ordered to take some horses and head North. It was imperative that the path they followed was always in sight of the Siberian railroad in case Japanese patrols mistook them for Russians. Burleigh spent his first night in the town of Pulantien dining on sardines and hard-boiled eggs. The next morning he covered a further 14 or so miles to Waufantein, a destroyed railway station, where he spent the night on the straw strewn floor of an empty building. It was at Waufantein that the Japanese eventual rout of the Russians had commenced; Burleighs path towards the front would now be scarred with the detritus of war, the rain had also laid bare many of the graves of the soldiers. Consequently, each nightly stop at the various railway stations he passed became more and more unbearable due to the heavy presence of flies. After they spent the night at the walled town of Kaiping, the weather changed for the worst, heavy thunderstorms and rain made the journey fraught with difficulty, they crossed many streams with water coming as high as the saddle flaps, and one of the company nearly drowned. The nights too were miserable, as they were spent in wet clothes. Eventually, the men reached the fighting front at Haicheng, where all the precautions observed in the face of the enemy were enforced. Three officers had been sent to them to act as guides, mentors and censors; they were strict in their duties. The men were invited to visit the General at his headquarters who welcomed them to the front of the second army. The correspondents impatiently waited for a sniff of the action that was occurring not far to the north, Burleigh wondered if he would ever get further than describing and chronicling the towns and villages he had passed through during the campaign, repeatedly being told by the Japanese, "very soon", "very sorry", so much so that it became a running joke amongst the correspondents. Around this time, Melton Prior commented, "even the stolid Burleigh is ready to return at any moment, for he feels he cannot do his duty conscientiously to his paper any more than I can. It is true we are at the front, with the enemy within 4 miles of us, but-and this is a very big "but"! -we are simply prisoners within the city walls, and if we very particularly wish to go outside we have to make special application, and an officer is sent to accompany us; but of course we are not allowed to go near the troops or outposts or see anything to write about or sketch. It is simply maddening."

Eventually, the correspondents received word that they must be up and ready to march to the site of the decisive battles for the town of Liaoyang; here the "excited schoolboys" witnessed the Japanese ready to spring into action, but only from a remote vantage point. The correspondents requested that the General allow them a closer view of the operations, as there was little to be had by looking at puffs of smoke and listening to the cannon from 4 miles away. The following night, four desperate correspondents surrendered to the inevitable and made up their minds to hand in their passes and leave Manchuria. Burleigh had a sneaking envy of them. A long series of bloodthirsty battles followed, with the Japanese eventually routing the Russians; the correspondents witnessed little of it. What Burleigh did see though was grim and sad, an episode he was glad to see the back of, estimating about 100,000 men of both sides dead after only a weeks worth of fighting, most of whom lay in the fields and streets where they fell.

During the early days of September 1904, after spending a few days wandering the town and locality, Burleigh, and nearly all the other correspondents left for Tokyo; there were other battles, but they too encompassed much of the same frustrations to the correspondents as Liaoyang. As he left to send his despatches, he had the feeling that the Japanese had studiously prevented him from doing his duty, and that this" leashed life of a war correspondent with the Japanese" was insupportable. He had wanted to witness their manner of conducting warfare and the personal side of the conflict, in reality, he got a panorama of a battle through long range field glasses and threats of the police if he disregarded their restrictions. This was not war reporting as he understood it. "If his rumblings at the general headquarters even slightly matched his complaints to Fleet Street he must have been an infernal nuisance". He wrote some lively stuff from behind the lines, but it was nothing like the old days of carrying messages from square to square. He had seen great days but in his view there was no future in it.

In the early days of January 1905, after fierce and prolonged battles of carnage in which Burleigh first acknowledged the large scale use of grenades and poison gas in warfare, Port Arthur fell to the Japanese, and although Burleigh was not there to witness it, he did offer to escort the wounded, no doubt to get eyewitness accounts, however he had to content himself with printing the second-hand accounts of others to conclude his book on the campaign. More battles were to take place between the two nations with peace eventually being signed in September 1905, which left the Japanese free to pursue their interests in Korea.

Chapter 8 - Other campaigns and incidents

By now, Burleigh had perhaps visited the scenes of war more than any other man of the age. This chapter focuses on some of the smaller, but more significant campaigns and events that he witnessed,

Greek / Turkish War, "The 30 Days War" 1897

As a "holiday" from Egypt and the Sudan, where Burleigh had been spending most of his time, he arrived in Athens in March 1897, for a five week sojourn to a country on the brink of war.

The Greco-Turkish War which was also known as the "Thirty Days War", was a war between Greece and the Ottoman Empire. Its immediate cause was Greek concern over the situation in Crete, where the Greek population was still under Ottoman control. The Greek army landed in Crete in order to liberate the island and unite it with Greece. Other European powers, however, intervened, and proclaimed Crete an international protectorate. This forced the Greek army to retreat to the mainland, from where it next attempted to advance northwards into Thessaly and Epirus. In Thessaly the Turks had concentrated six divisions of about 60,000 men under Edhem Pasha, with a seventh division joining a little later. The Greeks numbered just under 46,000, led by the inexperienced Crown Prince Constantine. The Greeks controlled the sea, outnumbering and outgunning the Turkish navy. Seeing that war was inevitable, Burleigh made his way from Athens to Thessaly.

In early April, Greek troops crossed the border, trying to start an uprising in Macedonia, and for a few days, much to Burleighs surprise, they carried all before them. Soon the armies met at Mati where the Greeks found themselves firmly in charge, but for some unknown reason, perhaps they assumed that the Turkish cavalry was on their heals, a panic ensued, and the army turned into a fleeing rabble. There were however no pursuing Turks, and it was hours after the troops had left that Burleigh himself decided to leave, seeing no sign of a pursuing enemy. The truth was he thought, that the Turks were so surprised at the disappearance of the Greeks, that they stayed put, fearing a trap.
Near Pharsala the Greeks tried to re-established order, but their morale failed, and they were only saved because the Ottoman Sultan ordered a cease-fire on May 20.

From a Larissa restaurant, the American correspondent, Palmer, reported, "In a Larissa restaurant one evening, after I had come in late from the field to file despatches, the group around a table included Bennet Burleigh, robustious of voice and form, who had often proved his gallantry, and a slender officer, attached to the Swedish Court, who was so meticulous in his politeness that he would rise with a bow to pass the salt.

"Think of that going under fire," said Burleigh. I was sitting next to Burleigh, and whispered to him, "He understands English just as well as he does French." The only sign that the Swede heard Burleighs slur appeared in two red spots in his cheeks.

The next day several members of the same group were approaching the battlefield under the protecting wall of a ridge which ran parallel to the infantry line. Burleigh and the Swede were leading … Burleigh and the Swede were slightly ahead of us. A few yards farther, and they would be completely exposed to the full sweep of the Turkish infantry fire over a Greek trench. Burleigh stopped.

"A war correspondent who is killed is no use to his paper," he said.

The Swede bowed from the hip. "If you will excuse me," he replied, "I should like a closer view of the infantry at work."

With spits of dust from bullets about his feet, I watched him, expecting every second to see him dropped, picking his way rather fastidiously over rough ground to the firing line. He was one of the men who have convinced me that there is such a thing as a charmed life.

Towards the end of the war, Burleigh entered the town of Volo, which was then occupied by the Turks. In order to avoid being detained, he riskily and secretly entered through the port at night, where he visited friends and acquaintances who informed him of Turkish atrocities, particularly amongst the irregulars. Some of the fellow correspondents he met there, who were travelling with the Turks, told him of being shot at by their own side in the midst of frenzied bloodlust. They also told him that his visit was an exceptional risk as, if captured he would be killed, prisoners it seemed were only taken under exceptional circumstances.

Peace was eventually signed on September 20, arranged by European powers. Turkey received a large amount of money as indemnification, and gained a small amount of land on the Thessaly border. This was the only occasion during the century of conflict between

Greece and the Turks in which Greece was forced to cede land to the Turks.

Burleigh had spent the campaign travelling with the Greeks, and at first, like most of the foreign correspondents, he was very biased towards their cause, however, he generally became disenchanted, branding Greek systems as corrupt and the people as having a frail morality. He wrote his account of the campaign, "The Greek War as I Saw It" in the "Fortnightly Review", where he concluded that the Greek King had made the war and was not forced into it for dynastic reasons, and that the Greeks could have beat the indifferent Turkish soldiers if they had been better managed, and finally, that the Greeks could pay their debts with proper financial management, whilst suggesting the need, but unlikelihood of foreign financial control.

Somaliland war 1903

Burleigh also reported the war in Somaliland against Muhammad bin Abdullah, the 'Mad Mullah'. After Queen Victoria's death (22nd Jan. 1901), imperial expansion virtually ceased and a period of consolidation took place. A minor expedition was taken to Somaliland in 1903. When Melton Prior arrived in camp he wrote, "approaching some tents saw a flag denoting "Post Office" and knowing that my dear old companion would not be far from there, I yelled," Burleigh", and in a moment he sprang off the bed, where he had been declining, and advanced with outstretched arms. How we welcomed one another I leave to the imagination." when Prior told him he had no supplies, because he thought he could get everything he wanted there, Burleigh replied "… there is not a camel to be had in the place… there is only sand… the shortest road to the public house is 1000 miles long." Ever resourceful, Burleigh arranged a friend of his to bring Prior some camels.

Burleigh and Prior started on an expedition from Behra to Bohotle across the River Houde, knowing that for several days there would be no possibility of obtaining water, so they drew a weeks worth, filling anything they could. They set off at 6.30 in the morning, slightly excited that they might meet a few of the enemy and come across a few wild beasts.

However, the riding was monotonous, the camels just kept plodding along at 2 1/2 miles an hour. Every so often the men would halt and examine a plant or an ant heap, or maybe just take a bit of whisky on board. After a day's ride they started out on a 72 mile march having to build their own protection in the form of a zereba for the night. A 3 hour watch was set up, to look out for wild beasts, particularly the impudent hyenas.

THE ABOVE SKETCH BY MELTON PRIOR, IS ENTITLED "BOER AND BRITON UNITED IN THE FIELD" AND SHOWS BURLEIGH PLAYING DRAUGHTS WITH A BOER COMMANDER AT OBBIA. PRIOR ADDED A NOTE TO THE SKETCH "YESTERDAY, IN COMPANY WITH BENNET BURLEIGH OF THE DAILY TELEGRAPH , I WALKED OVER TO THE BOER CAMP, WHERE I FOUND A BRITISH SOLDIER HAIL-FELLOW-WELL-MET, WITH HIS FORMER OPPONENT. A DRAUGHT BOARD MADE OF WATERPROOF SHEETING WAS LYING ON THE GROUND, AND BURLEIGH CHALLENGED A BOER COMMANDANT TO A GAME. THE TUSSLE ENDED IN A DRAW

The men had a comfortable first night, but on the second night, while Prior was in the middle of a happy dream, he was startled by the noise of a gunshot. Jumping out of bed, he then heard another shot. He reached for his pistol and hurried over to where Burleigh was, where he found him roaring with laughter, for he had just shot a hyena. It was a moonlit night, and Prior could see half a dozen of them sneaking around.

The following morning they set off and arrived in Damot, marching again the next day to their destination, having endured 130° heat in the coolest shade. Arriving at the encampment, they discovered that 230 British soldiers and followers had been surrounded by thousands of Somalis; The British were slaughtered, and the story of what had occurred had to be gleamed from the native camp followers.

The Times reported the Mullahs eventual peace terms "London, 1st December: Mr. Bennet Burleigh, the war correspondent of the "Daily Telegraph," is now on duty in Somaliland. He reports from Berbera that the Mad Mullah, Muhammad Abdullah, was once an interpreter on a British warship in East African waters. Mr. Burleigh states that letters have been lately received by the British authorities from the Mullah, offering to make peace on the condition that Great Britain will acknowledge his independence and grant him a seaport on the Gulf of Aden, east of Berbera."

Tripoli Italian Campaign

In 1909 Burleigh became seriously ill and thereafter, seemed old and weakened, he lacked his former energy and aplomb. This was in fact the first serious illness that had ever marred the unbroken course of Burleighs extraordinarily robust constitution. It brought him as near to the grave as any of his many perils in the field of battle. He made a slow recovery, but he was never the same man he had been before; the fire had departed out of his temperament, and he had lost all his pristine energy, audacious aplomb, and overpowering bonhomie. He was an old man; disease had finally discovered his age, a secret Burleigh had religiously concealed from all and sundry.

However, in 1911 Burleigh managed to make his way Tripoli, to commentate on Italy's war for the desert. There were many interests behind this war, the financial prosperity in Italy since 1900 made a large section of the nation anxious for the government to assert itself; The Banco di Roma had invested heavily in Tripoli, and complained bitterly of the obstacles thrown in its way by the Turks. The bank opened a branch in Tripoli, which became, to some extent, the cause of the war. The Turks saw it as an instrument of "peaceful penetration," which would be followed in due course by battleships. The bank did not fare well, and it became a question of war or bankruptcy. The Italians were also worried that the French, English and Germans would try and conquer Tripoli hence weakening their own security. On September 27th 1911, the Turkish Government was charged with the constant manifestation of hostility toward the legitimate activity of Italy in Tripoli, which the Turks rejected. The Italians started their invasion on October 3rd 1911. As in all wars, there are many facets, so to follow, are a few of the more notable that Burleigh wrote about. This war had a few notable firsts, it had the first mass wave of the new recruits to journalism, that is the war photographer, from Burleighs point of view, one could ask whether the imagination of the correspondent and his words were still necessary, when a photo could say a thousand words. This campaign is also noted for the first offensive use of aircraft. Just about 8 years since the first flights of the Wright brothers, on October 23rd, 1911, an Italian pilot flew over Turkish lines on a reconnaissance mission, and in 1912, the first ever bomb dropped from the air landed on Turkish troops in Libya.

General Caneva, the Italian commander in chief, told the Italian press how a doctor and accompanying soldier were asked to escort a wounded soldier, and how the accompanying soldier was forced to drive back the Arab crowd who were surrounding the carriage, the falling back of the crowd caused confusion and general flight causing rumours to spread that the town Arabs had risen and insurrection was afoot; a general panic ensued. The General told Burleigh, for the benefit of the English press, that there had been a deliberate revolt in the city, and that his soldiers had been fired upon and assailed from all angles. These and similar trifles, along with the apathy of Italian officers created a state of mind and panic which made a massacres of the natives in the oasis possible a few days later.

Of these massacres, Burleigh wrote (November 7th), "Steps have and are being taken to ensure greater tranquillity in Tripoli. The oasis of palms is being ruthlessly cleared of its population of villagers, small farmers and peasants. Very many have been killed and their corpses bestrew the fields and roads. The scent of war's scythe poisons the air. An aged Arab declares that 4000 have been slain, and with them at least 400 women and many children. Say half that number, and still you have a fearful, sanguinary monument of the horrors of war and the conquest,... Many have unquestionably been wantonly murdered. That is not always preventable in war, but in the 20th century, and in civilised warfare, it is quite without pale to shoot men and lads wholesale on sight without trial and because of their skin and dress."

Burleigh adds, " I have seen a crippled beggar - a man whose limbs were so deformed that he had to move by pushing along the ground in a sitting position - deliberately shot at near the Austrian Consulate. Dozens of other natives I have seen herded and corralled and others fired upon in broad daylight. But there are half a dozen colleagues, English and French and German - who assert that they have seen Arabs fusilladed in groups, and have even ' snap-shotted' instances where soldiers and officers indiscriminately fired upon these unfortunate natives. At any hour of the day you may see gangs of wretched natives being marched through the streets as prisoners. These are subsequently dealt with by the carabinieri, imprisoned - or otherwise. The daily captures effected in town and suburbs of men, women, and children run into hundreds, nay thousands."

The censor was at work again in Tripoli, and refused one of Burleigh's telegrams, which said, "Though the disembarkation of the Italian troops on October 12th had been conducted with very creditable efficiency and speed, British marines could probably, owing to their greater experience in such matters, conduct it even better". The censor rejected it because it stated that British were better than Italians, and he only wanted praise for the Italians.

By October 18th 1912, the war was over; a peace treaty was signed, handing over the provinces that Italy had started the war in order to control.

A fellow correspondent remarked that he felt that this campaign was the swansong of Burleighs career. A weary Titan, his age and a recent illness, sapping an energy that in the past had seemed unfathomable, and denying his efforts attain superiority in the field.

Balkan Peninsula

Burleigh had originally visited the Balkan peninsula through the crisis which followed the overthrow of Sultan Abdul Hamid by the Young Turks in the mid 1870's. He sympathised with the Serbian aspirations which gained him the enduring affection of the people. Despite his illness Burleigh had not discarded his profession. He returned to the Balkans in 1912, after Bulgaria and Serbia had mobilized in response to Montenegro declaring war on Turkey. This was to be a significant war and journey for Burleigh, he was now aged around 73, and it was here that he saw his

last shots fired in war.
Chapter 9 - Between the wars.
Part A- News from the home front.

Burleigh was also a hard working and popular reporter in the intervals between wars. In Empire of east Burleigh said "War is terrible and cruel", and that he himself was a lover of peace, and consequently he took many civil causes under his wing.

In 1880, public excitement was running very high over the efforts of a certain Mr Bradlaugh to enter the House of Commons. Mr Bradlaugh had been elected the MP for Northampton and refused to take his oath on the Bible, he was however determined to take his place on the benches. It was thought he would try to enter the chamber, and that there was bound to be a scene in the lobby of the House into which no reporters could hope to gain access. Burleigh found some clothing, a ladder and the tools of a gas fitter, and went to work on the lights in the lobby. Sure enough, Bradlaugh entered the chamber in a struggle and Burleigh had the excellent vantage point from the top of his ladder. The following day, to the perplexity of the MPs, the news made an interesting headline. This was not an unusual turn for Burleigh, some reports claim that Burleigh had turned up at some official receptions dressed in a seedy frock-coat, posing as an American senator.

Burleigh would have been quite a wealthy man; during the Boer War, Winston Churchill was earning £250 per month as a correspondent, and then adding the income from his books and lecture tours, he earned about £4000 in 10 months. The average yearly salary for a skilled man at the time was about £55. In fact when he died, Burleighs will dated 7th November 1914, left a personal estate of £1331 3*s*. 10*d* to his second wife, including an annuity of 10 shillings a week to his daughter Bernice Gordon Burleigh, who was an infant at the time. However, an announcement in the London Gazette of 20th August 1915 called for creditors to claim against Burleighs estate, and it seems there was a court case, May v Burleigh 1915. This case may have been lost given the reports that his second wife was seen begging in London during her later years.

A reporter from The Times remarked in his biography the first time he saw of "what cool material Bennet Burleigh was made". He had been sent to investigate an explosion at the rocket factory in Woolwich Arsenal towards the end of 1883. Whilst the said reporter was trying to gain access to the factory, just after lunch, and being denied access on any account by the gatekeeper, he saw Burleigh, marching through the gates unmolested within a procession of workmen as one of themselves.

CUT FROM THE FILM FOOTAGE OF IAN HISLOPS BBC DOCUMENTARY "SCOUTING FOR BOYS" IN WHICH BURLEIGH SAT BACK LEFT IN THE CARRIAGE CAN BE SEEN WAVING HIS HAT AND CELEBRATING DURING BADEN POWELLS "HEROIC DEFENDER OF MAFEKING" HOMECOMING CELEBRATION.

It is said that the British are obsessed with the weather, writing in 1906, as a guest contributor amongst several other eminent travellers, on the question of the British climate being maligned, Burleigh wrote, "of climate we have none, of weather a superabundance. My wife reminds me that but recently there was within the period of twenty four hours the round of the four seasons of the year. Speaking for myself, as a globe ranger, ... Where, the world round, can you see such grass and green fields?"

In 1911, Burleigh was to organise a memorial for his friend Melton Prior, who had died during the previous November. Burleigh however was called away by the Italian campaign in Tripoli, so he passed his papers to a Mr Watson of the Times in order that he carry on the work . In Priors memory, Burleighs wife sculptured a memorial plaque, a life size bronze medallion set in onyx. She had travelled all over London but ended up travelling to Paris to find the exact material she wanted. She initially worked on the medallion in clay, finally coming up with an apt piece which is displayed in St Paul's Cathedral. Burleigh himself was no stranger to such realisations, he had his own wax figure on display in

Madame Tussauds.

KINNAIRD HALL, DUNDEE,
MONDAY, 28th SEPTEMBER, 1885.

ADMISSION Reserved Seats, 2/-, Second Seats, 1/-, Back Seats, 6d

Tickets and Plan at Methven, Simpson, & Co's, 112 Nethergate
Doors open at 7.30; commence at 8.

SAD SOUDAN.

Mr Bennet Burleigh

("Daily Telegraph" War Correspondent on the)

True Story of the Terrible Soudan Campaign.

Despite his strangely modified Glasgow accent, Burleigh also ran a line in after dinner speaking; On 28th September 1885, a poster advertises that, Bennet Burleigh War Correspondent of the "Daily Telegraph" was to give a presentation in Dundee's Kinnaird Hall on the war in Sudan. This show also toured several other venues. Some of the praiseworthy extracts from the press notices follow; they provide an interesting insight into the personality and social standing of Burleigh:

"It has been jokingly said that when a newspaper Editor has to send out a war correspondent he looks down the list of his staff, and then selects the most worthless man for the post - one he can well afford to lose, and can easily replace if he gets killed. A moments contemplation of Mr Burleigh will prove this to be inaccurate. He is a singularly modest man, so much so, indeed, that I found so little difficulty in extracting from him certain facts which are given below. His gaze is frank and honest, and his manner gentle, but his frame is powerful and well-knit; and his close cut features, his determined mouth, and firm, massive jaw, are so impressive that I instantly decided to be extremely careful not to annoy him in any way. - Mr Burleigh Interviewed" - Pall Mall Gazette.

"A pleasant frank face, tanned where "the fierce sun overhead laughed his pitiless laugh"; keen eyes; a forehead with the perceptive facilities well developed; of medium height, with broad shoulders, and arms whose muscles are "as strong as iron bands;" with a square chin indicative of firmness; Mr Bennet Burleigh, the well known War Special of the "Daily Telegraph" fulfils in his person and appearance the impressions gleaned from his writings, of one who could ride all day and write all night" - Society.

"Mr Bennet Burleigh, who is Scotch by birth, has had great military experience, having served as an officer in the Confederate Army during the Civil War in the United States, where he was twice wounded, twice taken prisoner, and even sentenced to death. In the campaign against Arabi, Mr Burleigh was exceptionally successful, and sent home the first account of the victory of Tel-el-Kebir. He then rode seventy miles across the desert in Cairo, and, on being refused permission to send off a telegram from there, returned alone across the desert to Tel-el-Kebir. Mr Burleigh was specially mentioned in an official despatch for conspicuous bravery in the Sudan, being the first and only correspondent ever honoured in this way." - Lloyds News.

"Mr Burleigh is a remarkable man. He is physically and mentally strong, a man of immense daring and resource." - Ipswich Free Press.

"The telegrams and letters sent by him from the battlefield to the "Daily Telegraph" during the past war created much remark. Mr Burleigh was mentioned in the "London Gazette" for conspicuous bravery, by order of the Commander in Chief" - Queen.

"A Scotchman, forty two years of age, 5 feet 9 inches "in his camps," with a John Bull jowl, a larking devil in his eye, and the air and spirit of a soldier. Burleigh is a favourite in camp, the club, or columns of the "largest circulation". Enough to say that he lectures as well as he writes. We heard him for two hours, and thought time had stolen one and a half of them from us. Two lines sum up his performance on the platform :- list his discourse of war, and you shall hear a fearful battle rendered you in music." - Irish Times, Dublin.

"Private Woods, of the 1st Grenadier Guards, in whose arms Colonel Burnaby breathed his last, was loud in his praise of at least one of the correspondents, and said that Mr Bennet Burleigh, although, "only a civilian" fought with much bravery." - Morning Advertiser.

"Last night, at St James Great Hall, Mr Bennet Burleigh delivered a lecture on the Sudan campaign before a large audience, and proved himself and excellent lecturer carrying his hearers with unbroken interest throughout his story." - Morning Post.

"Mr B.G. Burleigh of the "Daily Telegraph", is a gentleman of whom it has been said that had he been a soldier during the Sudan War, instead of a journalist, he would have had the Victoria Cross for the gallantry he displayed in the desert battles notably in that of Abu Kru." - Norwich Argus.

"That Mr Bennet Burleigh, the "Daily Telegraph's" Special Correspondent in the late Sudan War, has dared to undertake to tell the true story of that Campaign, has raised ire in military circles. The truth will now out, and it will lose nothing in effect by waiting." - Paris Morning News.

"Burleigh, the "Special" gave a capital lecture on the Desert Campaigns. Many soldiers who have arrived in time, testify to his personal gallantry. The Daily Telegraphs representative is assuredly the "Boss Special"."- Sunday Times.

"Mr Bennet Burleigh in a lecture last evening in St James Hall, severely criticised the measures taken by the late Government for the relief of General Gordon." - Globe. (Second notice)

"Mr Burleighs lecture contains some stories of the campaigning in those dark lands, which the censorship of the Press has hitherto concealed from the public" - Englishman

"The lecture was a very satisfactory bit of work, and if Mr Burleigh proposes to run it about the country it will "go"." - World.

"Very good, "when the Hurly Burleighs done, we shall know how the battles were lost and won"... - Funny Folk.

"The lecture which was delivered by Mr Bennet Burleigh, ... is a valuable contribution to history". - Manchester Guardian.

Burleigh did not just limit himself to lectures on the Sudan; for presentation in the Olympia in London circa 1897-8, Burleigh had written "The Mahdi, or for the Victoria Cross", a jingoistic and patriotic spectacle of the stage. This huge show was presented by Barnum and Bailey, the American circus company, and boasted visits by all the members of the Royal Family. The show consisted of two heavy set scenes, each covering about 7,000 square yards of canvas, 3 stages and 3 rings. There were mosques, towers, fortified cities, rivers, mountains, and forests all depicting the Upper Nile. The show was a military piece and pictured camp life and battles in the Sudan. A hundred Sudanese, of various tribes fresh from their native land, had been injected into the play, which employed about 600 people. Among these were 100 English cavalrymen from the Royal Reserve and two batteries of artillery. Apparently, the raw natives from the east presented a distinct entertainment in themselves, in their curious costumes, camp trappings, arms, religious rites and pastoral games. In the battles which ensued between the natives and the British troops, the infantry, cavalry and artillery seemed to hotly engage, and as if this was not enough to furnish the necessary noise and excitement, a gunboat from the Nile also played a part in the melee. There were bombardments. cavalry charges, artillery practice and hand-to-hand engagements of the most bloodthirsty character, the British forces getting into action forming one of the most thrilling scenes ever placed upon a stage. The show was admired by the critics of the day as a being an admirable display.

In his notes regarding the show, Burleigh believed that the only way to show the toils and dangers involved in the struggle between civilisation and barbarism, was to accurately reproduce the characteristic scenes that occurred during the Sudan campaign. The strong, fanatical following of the professed prophet, "The Mahdi", courted death and paradise with mad haste. Burleigh honoured the British soldiers who withstood their onslaughts, as Mahdism was determined not just to conquer their own lands, but also those of Mecca, Constantinople, and the rest of the world. Burleigh adds that the show was based on real events, with only the time, place and groupings being slightly changed for dramatic representation.

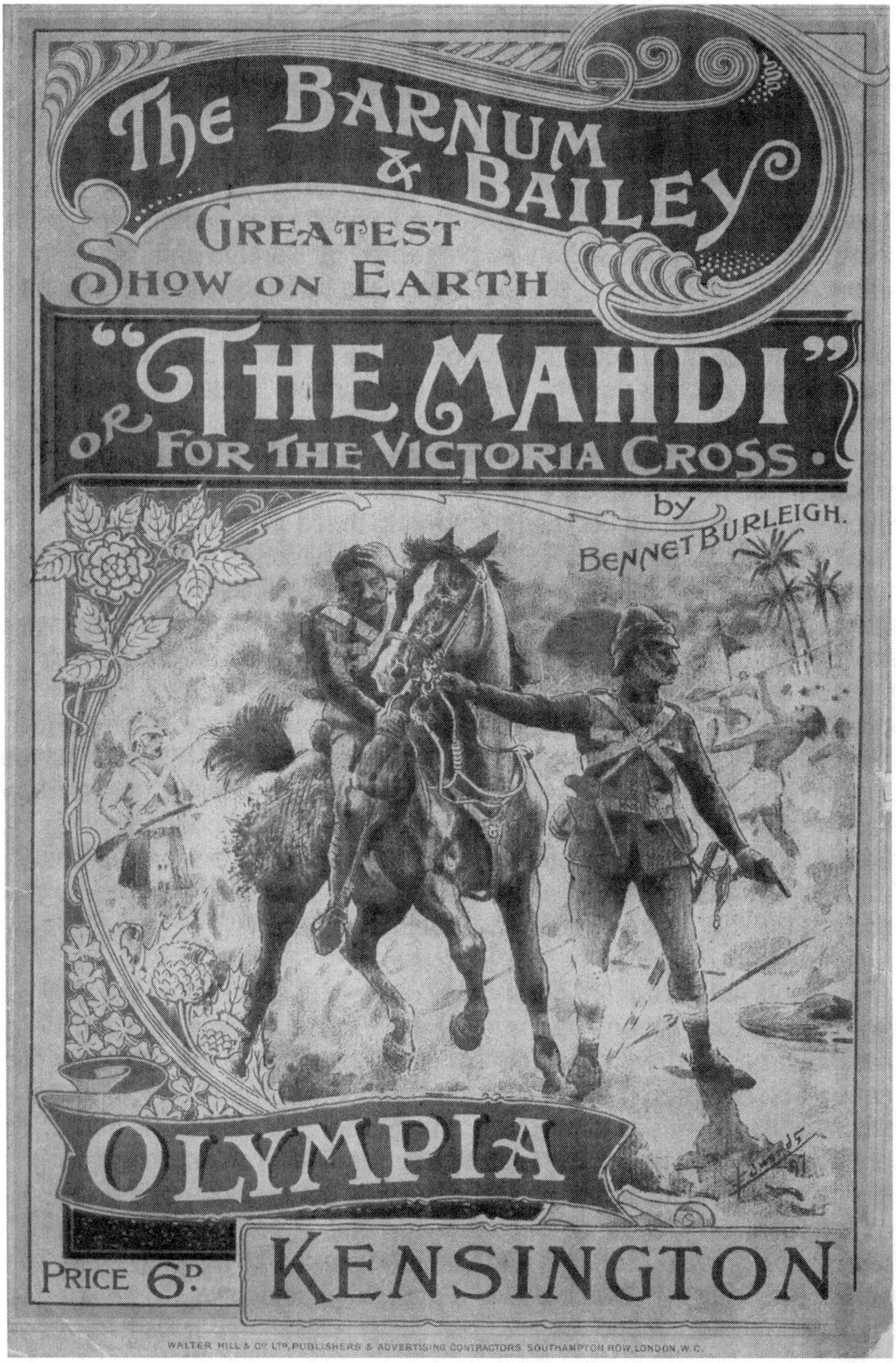
The Barnum & Bailey
Greatest Show on Earth
"The Mahdi"
or For the Victoria Cross.
by Bennet Burleigh.
Olympia
Price 6d.
Kensington
WALTER HILL & CO. LTD, PUBLISHERS & ADVERTISING CONTRACTORS, SOUTHAMPTON ROW, LONDON, W.C.

COPY OF THE SHOWS PROGRAMME COVER.

    The show proceeded as follows; Scene 1 is set in the afternoon until moonlight on the banks of the upper Nile. A native marriage is taking place at a Holy place, and there is much singing and dancing. The whole affair is being observed by British and American officers, accompanied by their wives and betrothed, who are in the process of travelling up the Nile from Cairo; the Westerners are unaware of plans by Mahdist emissaries for a general uprising, and the slaughter of the Christians of Lower Egypt. A local sheik had for some time been enamoured with one of the Western ladies in the group, and had resolved to abduct her; both he and his men, had been working as donkey boys and servants to the Westerners, awaiting their moment. During the celebrations the sheik recognises the Mahdi's emissaries, and introduces himself, consenting, along with his followers, to assist them as they proclaim the Mahdi has come. During the height of the Moslems celebrations, the sword is drawn as the sheik proclaims the true Mahdi has comes. The tourist attempt to retreat from the scene, but they are quickly surrounded, and the ladies are dragged away up through a ravine towards the Dervish camp at Suakin. The remaining Western officers take to pursuing them.

    Scene 2 takes place in the Dervish camp, again there are great celebrations, including jugglers, feats of strength and camel racing as the Mahdi rides in and takes his place in the chief hut, where he proceeds to hand out rewards and punishments. As the captors enter the camp with the ladies, they endeavour to take them to their private quarters, but are told that women of their class must first be presented before the Mahdi; thus preserving their dignity for the moment. The Dervish Calvary announce a large force of British troops approaching, which causes a general flight and panic, with the ladies being hurriedly taken away. This is followed by a grand and imposing entry by the regular British Sudan Army, and a fight ensues between them and the Dervish rear guard.

    In scene 3, the location changes again, it is dawn in a small Arab town on the banks of the Upper Nile. As the regular days work commences for the natives, we see the ladies being taken for safe keeping to a large house near the mosque. The British are not far behind and launch a general assault on the town, but the first wave is repelled, only to be saved in the nick of time by reinforcements, including most of the officers from the first scene. The Dervish take shelter within the town and shoot at the British from buildings, with cannons being needed to take down the walls, a Nile gun boats enters the affray, and its guns boom and rattle throughout the town. A desperate fight ensues from house to house, and one of the ladies is spotted waving her white hanky from the window of the large house. Some of the original officers from scene 1, enter the house as a wall is demolished by a chance shell from the gun boat. Through the dust, we see one of these officers fighting like a caged lion to protect the women from their Dervish captors until they are slain or escape. Once freed, the captives are then led outside, along with the brave, but mortally wounded protecting officer. As his life ebbs, his friends surround him, and the betrothed of one of the rescued ladies, who had previously won the Victoria Cross, places it on the dying mans chest, to show him that never a braver man had won the decoration. The dying man comprehends the act, and raises his hand to the cross, his duty nobly done, his life closed in honour and glory, and with his last breath he cries "God Save the Queen!". - Curtain.

Part B - Burleigh the liberal imperialist.

The industrial, communications and bureaucratic "revolutions" in Britain between 1750 and 1850 gave the state the incentive to extend its protection to the poorest and most vulnerable members of society. During the latter stages of Victoria's reign, social reforms to combat problems such as poverty and unemployment were widely discussed and acted upon. Many historians argue that these liberals set the scene for the eventual creation of the Welfare State. Burleigh himself wrote and promoted many liberal values on subjects as diverse as unemployment and old age pensions. He was also the treasurer for a society based in Islington to get the working man the vote.

Burleigh, like many people associated with the Daily Telegraph at the time, could be described as a bohemian, locally described as people who were not quite starving in the garret, but people who mixed with hard drinking, raffish, matrimonially complicated actors, artists and writers. Burleigh was a member of the Savage Club, a select club, though its members were not particularly wealthy; it was really a place where members could meet for food and drink, to discuss work and life, and be entertained. It is remarked in their history that Burleigh used to turn up at the conclusion of some war or other, full of life and high in spirits, but also having a craving for getting out there again to some fresh war. Big celebrations were quite common upon the return of these correspondents who had literally returned from the jaws of death, and with good reason, as the loss of life among correspondents was out of all proportion to the loss of life of regular troops.

When not on foreign duty, Burleigh was also the chairman of the United Democratic Club in London. As a member was to describe it, it "was the resort of all those who gave life and being to the advanced movements of the Metropolis. Here assembled those daring spirits who would have ventured on any enterprise, from editing the Times to commanding the Channel Fleet. And yet, alas! ... the Committee were so unbusinesslike, ... that while they aspired to revolutionise the world, they had not the ability to run a whelk stall." Some prominent members of the club, apart from the sprinklings of republicans, nationalists and anarchists, included Karl Marx's daughter and the Daughter of William Morris; thanks to the variety of its members, the club was never boring, holding renowned lectures, dinners and concerts.

Another guest at the Democratic club recalls, just as in Kipling's Torpenhow, the guest could see in Burleigh his way of "taking hold of a man and making him do things". He describes one situation in the early 1890's, when he was dragged down to a lunch at the Democratic Club and not permitted to leave by Burleigh until he had become a member of the club; a few weeks later he found himself along with Burleigh on the committee.

Another guest and his wife recalled meeting Burleigh, who he first saw whilst waiting on the tables at a Saturday night house dinner. After being introduced, Burleigh led them to a large room, saying, "there is no ceremony here. Make yourself comfortable; hang your things where you can. I will return to you when dinner is served." This guest from the provinces, was fairly shocked as he mingled with those waiting for dinner, "It was the first time we had been in Bohemia, or had seen women under seventy years of age indulging in the weed." Burleigh shortly returned, and as chairman asked the new guests to take a seat next to him at the table of honour.

The unique environment of the Democratic Club led it to become the "Behind the Scenes" source of many of the outstanding labour events that were later to play out on a much larger stage, such as the problems with unemployment and pensions; subjects that Burleigh was to lecture upon. However, due to defaults on the payment of subscriptions, the club was eventually wound up.

In his pamphlet, " The Unemployed", 1887, he argued that the unemployed can be classified as those who need work but cannot find it, and those who need not find work nor try to. He goes onto say that both classes are very numerous, but it is mainly with the former, and their condition, that one should be most concerned. He goes on to say that it is the 'have nots' who are using the improved machinery of the time for social and political agitation in order to demand the reasonable proposition of the more honest of them for "work or bread". He believed that the growth in wealth was not divided or levelled out equally amongst the capitalists and the day labourer, in fact it heightened the inequalities between them, and amongst the working class, privation was widespread. Since 1883 during each recurring winter the people in the cities had become familiarised with unemployed agitation; the crowds included clerks and mechanics who were unhappy to spend six pence on foetid lodging houses and begged for shelter. On 7th October 1887, the agitators raised a red flag in Trafalgar Square, promising work and bread. The publicity given to the agitators by the press increased the number of their followers who claimed that the wealth they produced as labourers gave them a right to bread. A programme of relief works were suggested, for example, the council could employ the poor directly for repairing roads or erecting bathhouses and ensure that fair rents were paid for fair properties. "Three months of beef-tea and generous diet, and the opportunity to earn his living, have oftentimes resuscitated many an apparent wastrel". The police started to pay more attention to the red meetings, almost to the point of causing political agitation. The liberal arguments raged, that a sense of justice was lost at the sight of thousands of hungry men and women, capable of work, and demanding work / bread in vain; "you cannot decry them as 'the unwashed' when modern urban life denies them baths"; they continued, "ministers… can find millions for war at a few hours notice. Society cannot afford to let these people perish in the street". Burleigh concluded his work; "Employment and cosy homes will provide greater stability to the state than law courts and the police … On the grounds of economy, prudence and humanity new methods must be adopted for dealing with the unemployed".

Burleigh, did not limit his views and ideals to the printed word, he was a man of action and made his voice heard in other ways. Along the Strand one Sunday afternoon in November 1887, on a protest march to Trafalgar Square, the police attacked an unarmed crowd with their batons in the so called defence of law and order, Burleigh for his part was arrested on the charge of being a loose, idle, and disorderly person, disturbing the peace with intent to cause a felony; it seems he had threatened to knock down the first policeman who touched him. Burleigh, who was sworn in as a Presbyterian at Bow Street Magistrates Court, claimed he was actually in the process of obeying the orders of the police to move on; the charge was dropped and an apology made to Burleigh. Before a year had passed, Trafalgar Square became a recognised place for public meetings.

Burleigh wasn't always just involved in protest marches, on June 22nd 1887, Burleigh along with a Mr Helby of the London School Board led a children's procession of about 13,000 to Hyde Park, the day being arranged by Lawson of the Daily Telegraph, in honour of Queen Victoria's Golden Jubilee. The day proceeded with a fête of sports, games, food, theatre and dancing. Later in the day the children received commemoration medals, and the Queen undertook a procession.

In 1889, Burleigh wrote under the pseudonym, "a friend of the poor", and used the pages of the Daily Telegraph to champion their cause; he highlighted the poor housing conditions in the East End and helped a number of slum residents mount legal challenges against their landlords. His original investigation had been into the working conditions of females but he soon realised that their work place was usually also their home, and he was appalled at the sanitary conditions therein.

Montagu Williams QC reminisces in his biography on a case brought by Burleigh and others. This case was in regard to 3 properties in Shoreditch, which consisted of 33 rooms and accommodated 108 people. Despite the properties having being recently condemned as the result of a previous court case, which was appealed by the owners on the promise that they would put them into a proper state of repair, the terrible ventilation, damp and vermin problems in the small rooms continued. Williams took on the case and decided to visit the properties himself; once there, he met for the tour with Burleigh and several others. After the viewing, he commented - "To think that one's fellow-creatures were doomed to live in such filthy holes!" On the advice of the sanitary officers who claimed that the buildings were beyond repair, Williams QC ordered that the property be vacated and demolished. A catch 22 situation then occurred: having demolished the housing, it left the tenants homeless! Obviously such a situation couldn't be tolerated, and eventually Burleigh and others set up the Fair Rents for Healthy Homes League, whose policy it was to threaten the naming and shaming of the slum landlords via the press. This course prompted swift action, as Burleigh happily announced in the Daily Telegraph of Christmas 1889, that the East End was a flurry of whitewashing, roof mending, plastering and pointing; however, he also considered, that whether, despite the paint, these homes were still little more than burial vaults.

Throughout these years 1885 - 1896, a newspaperman, Joseph Burgess, remembers Burleigh having a burning ambition to become an M.P.. Burleigh was always fiercely proud of his Glasgow roots, and fought for three elections there, but always unsuccessfully. Despite working for a Conservative newspaper, Burleigh was a self-declared advanced radical and socialist. He stood in the Lanarkshire and Glasgow constituencies—in 1885 as Liberal-Labour candidate, and in 1886 as Liberal Unionist, but

Sketches around Bethnal-Green. by our Special Artist

A Match box maker taking home work 2 Gross of Boxes Price 5ᵈ

Mr Bennet Burleigh The Daily Telegraph's "A Friend of the Poor"

An Inhabitant

Some of the Condemned Houses

Turning Mahogany Table legs at 4ᵈ the set of four

165

his credentials were attacked by his opponents, who brought up the fact that he had been engaged in piracy around Detroit in his youth.

Burleigh later sued a fellow candidate for slander who claimed that he had been convicted of assault in Glasgow in 1869, but was himself then counter sued; Burleigh won the case and was awarded £500, but the costs of fighting and losing the election came to about £350, so he made little gain.

The closest he came to winning a seat occurred in the 1892 election which he lost by just 159 votes. He stood for the Scottish Parliamentary Labour Party, for his hometown Tradeston seat, standing for "the complete overthrow of injustice, privilege and monopoly, and the co operative ownership by the workers of the land and means of production", but again failed, after being labelled a "Unionist journalist". This was perhaps to do with his involvement, or rather the lack of it, in the recently formed Postmen's Union.

Despite not realising his political ambitions, Burleigh still enjoyed politics and his role as a friend of the poor. In 1908, he delivered "An address on old age pensions", for the National Liberal Club, which was later published. In the speech, he argued that the time was right to offer pensions as a matter of state policy because the plight of the aged poor was great. He argued, that regardless of what type of scheme was to be forthcoming, it was a moral obligation to recognise the debt owed by the state to these people. It was his hope that the workhouses could be emptied of the aged poor, and that they could keep the roof over their heads, enjoying the company of family and friends. He then harked back to his election address of the 1880's in which he pinned his faith that "the workers were entitled to be well fed, well clad, well lodged, with sufficient provision for old age". Burleigh then described how the pension systems of other countries worked, and speculated on how much the pension should be, coming up with a figure of 5 shillings for subsistence, but not under 7 shillings would be better. Then Burleigh presents the types of pension systems available, arguing the pros and cons of contributory and non contributory schemes, including thrift schemes, state insurance, a universal pension, and a way of measuring the deserving, before he presents his own scheme, in which he suggests the scheme should be a civil right, automatically received, and earned as a kind of back pay funded through a direct tax of 1% on the nations wealth rather than for instance, through a charity or workhouse dole. He argued that the country could afford it given its recent huge growth in wealth with the same population; adding that in 1840 per capita wealth was £20, and now (1908) it was £50 per head. He concludes, that the paying of a pension would have so many direct and indirect benefits to a society, bringing hope and comfort to people, as well as improving sanitary conditions and housing stock. In the same year, it seemed that the press of the day were not immune to mocking Burleigh; A spoof article pictures Burleigh the correspondent present at the siege Troy, the "newspaper" claims that news has reached them of his condition, claiming that Burleighs "monotonous and wearisome fidelity to his post has prematurely aged him to such an extent that he has been frequently mistaken for Nestor" - (a brave orator and elder during the Trojan Wars, 110 years old, and a man who often liked to give advice to the younger warriors.)

Part C - Family Life

Bennet Burley had his first child on 22nd February 1861 at the age of 20. The child was named Marion Scott Burley; she later took on the married name Summerhill, (it is from this child that the the author is descended). Marion was born illegitimately in Lord Darnley's cottage, located in the shadow of Glasgow Cathedral. A month later, on March 22nd, the happy couple took their Banns according to the formalities of the United Presbyterian Church and were married, thus legitimising the child. Burley had married Marion Thomson, a seamstress and daughter of John Thomson, a House Factor from Glasgow. A House Factor is an old Scottish name, the modern equivalent being an estate agent or rent collector. Scott was the maiden name of Marion Thomsons mother who also happened to be called Marion. Several months after the child was born, Burley left for America and the Civil War. He returned home after his trial in Port Clinton, and decided he wanted to become a journalist, so he went back to America to learn his trade. At first he worked for a newspaper in Texas and wanted his family to join him there though it seems they were unwilling, so he returned to the British Isles, and moved to Dublin for a while where his daughter was to receive her education.

In 1871, both Marion and her young daughter were back in Glasgow and living with an elder sister. It seems by now that the relationship had broken down and Burleigh had deserted her. The continuing story of Marion the elder is quite sad and tragic. She died aged 42 on June 25th 1884 in the City Poorhouse, Glasgow. She had been admitted as a pauper, a former sewing machinist, and still the wife of newspaper correspondent Bennet Burleigh. She eventually succumbed to Uterine disease (hysteria) and Plithisis Pulmonalis or T.B., with the death being witnessed by her son in law William Burrows.

In an article in the Manchester Evening News, celebrating Marions fiftieth wedding anniversary in 1939, she said she had met her husband when she arrived to visit a relative in Sauchiehall Street, Glasgow; at this time she was already a young widow with 5 children and was introduced to her future husband Isaac by his mother who she had been chatting to on the boat she had taken to get there. The couple were married within 7 weeks. In the article, it seems she was so very proud of her father, mentioning the fact that he was the only correspondent to ever be handed a Generals despatch, that of General Stewart in Egypt, which he had to take to Cairo. The same newspaper later reported her obituary;

copied here in full, as her families legends add something special as to who the real Bennet Burleigh was; "Mrs Marion Scott Summerhill, placid daughter of a "wild" father - the late Bennet Burleigh famous war correspondent and friend of Winston Churchill has died in her home in Oldham Road, Failsworth aged 83. Mrs Summerhill, the eldest daughter of Burleigh contrasted her fathers nature completely. While he was dodging cannon fire in the South African war, she was writing poetry or taking long country walks. She called her father a wild, wild man, her husband 78 year old Mr Isaac Summerhill said today.

BURLEIGHS FIRST DAUGHTER MARION (CENTRE) WITH HER HUSBAND ISSAAC, AND DAUGHTERS (L-R) SARAH, MADONNA (AUTHORS GREAT GRAN), FLORENCE, ANABELLE, AND ETHEL (FRONT) CHILD UNKNOWN.

Bennet Burleigh went out in 1884 with the Gordon Relief

Expedition, and in 1895 with the Ashanti Expedition. During that time he was with Winston Churchill who was a young war correspondent. One of Bennet Burleighs first assignments was in Madagascar where the French were having some trouble. To avoid capture by the enemy he walked over 100 miles through one of the roughest parts of the island. He was in the Spanish Riff Campaign in Morocco and the Graeco- Turkish war, and was on good terms with Kitchener at Khartoum. He also knew Rudyard Kipling. During the Boer War, he complained that censorship robbed him of his descriptive style. Mrs Summerhill was born in Glasgow and educated in Ireland. She came to Lancashire with her family who started a business in Failsworth."

The Manchester Evening News adds that when Mrs Summerhill fell ill in the 1920's, she received a letter of sympathy and a wheelchair from her towns and the then Oldham M.P. Winston Churchill which the family cherish. There was also mention of another family legend that discusses the possibility that Burleigh had a significant amount of shares in a South African gold / diamond mine that were lost and never cashed in!

With regard to Churchill being the M.P. for Oldham, another interesting letter appeared in the Churchill archives; this letter is from the then proprietor of the Daily Telegraph, E. Lawson, and is dated 10th December 1936, which was written to Churchill's then secretary, Miss Pearman. Lawson states that he had received a letter from Burleighs eldest daughter, Marion Burleigh, (the authors family link to Burleigh), and having made further enquiries in Manchester, "there seems to be no doubt that she is genuinely the daughter of Bennet Burleigh by his first marriage, Actually she was the illegitimate daughter, legitimised by the subsequent marriage of her parents. That possibly would account for having no record of her. She is undoubtedly perfectly genuine, and having warned you in my previous letter, I thought I had better let you have this information. We are sending her a small amount of money"; quite why Churchill was warned about her is unfortunately unknown.

In the 1870s Burleigh had moved to New York and on the 9th of January 1873, in Manhattan Burleigh committed bigamy and married for the second time. His younger bride was called Marion Elizabeth Shearer and she had been born around 1852 in Leeds, the daughter of John Shearer and Elizabeth Martin.

Burleigh and Marion soon had a daughter, Chrissie, who was born in New York in 1875 and later, a son, Sherer born in 1877, who during his later life returned to America to live in Arkansas with his wife Martha; The physical description of Sherer on the immigration documents stated that he had a 'misplaced toe on his right foot'. In 1878, Burleigh senior returned to England and census details for 1881 had him living in Lambeth, Surrey. Here he shared a house with his wife Marion, his daughter Maria aged five months who had been born in Brixton, and his father whose occupation was regarded as a merchant/importer, who was now widowed and aged 74. Burleighs father Robert eventually died in 1902 at the grand old age of 96. In a show of love for his father, he transcribed the following verse in the fly leaf of his gifted copy of "Two Campaigns" - "To the protector of my infancy, the guide and companion of my youth and manhood, My Father from his son, Bennet Burleigh."

Another child, Beatrice was later born in England in 1886. The 1891 census sees him living in Clapham with wife Marion, son Sherer, now 14, and daughters Maria, 10 and Beatrice, 5. However, Marion died young aged 43, and was buried in Norwood Cemetery, Lambeth, on 29th April 1895. It also seems, that given the dates of birth of the children in his second family and third families, that the couple were by this time somewhat estranged, however, a lot of the census information I have looked at does not seem particularly accurate.

After the untimely death of Marion, Burleigh married for the third time in 1898 to an artist, Bertha Preuss, who was originally from Varsovis, Poland. They had (according to the 1901 UK census) six children - four sons: Robert b.1893; Bennet b. 1894; James b.1897; Bertie b.1898; and two daughters: Beatrice b.1886 (daughter of Marion) and Bertha b.1892 and they resided in Battersea. In a remark made to his granddaughter by a member of the family, when she was young, it seems that her father, Bertie, was their only legitimate child

Burleigh's daughter Bertha, wrote several books in later life, one was called "An Artist At The Zoo" which contained her musings and drawings of zoo creatures. This interest in animals was fostered by her father, who at various times brought back from his world travels an exciting collection of "beasties" and other memorabilia. On one occasion Burleigh brought home a Bush Baby which he had kept as a pet in Africa. It was a knowing creature which slept in his coat pocket, but unfortunately the cold British weather was too much for it. After the Sudan campaigns he brought back war trophies, such as Emirs flags and weapons which were displayed in an exhibition at the Kelvingrove Museum, Glasgow. He also once presented 2 Spanish terrapins from Mellila, North Africa to the Zoological Society of London.

Burleigh used to tell his children a story about his friend, the War Artist, Melton Prior. Prior was resting on the hot African desert sands when an ostrich suddenly spying his bald head, and mistaking it for her egg, started to settle down on it. Startled, he jumped up and ran on his short legs for his dear life, with the ostrich after him all worked up at the thought of losing her egg, which promptly disappeared into a cloud of dust. Bertha was so talented an artist that Rudyard Kipling (with whom she later sat on the WW1 war graves commission) thought Bertha would be the best artist to illustrate his works, such as the Jungle Book. When WW1 broke out, she was a journalist for "The Queen", and passed through the German lines that had been drawn around Brussels on foot, reporting that the German people needed a good whipping if the world were to ever be at peace. On her return though, she could not get across the channel from Belgium, so ended up crossing it in an open boat. She did eventually return to the continent, and went to France as a correspondent; She returned to Britain in 1915 and lectured for the British Government, finding herself in Ireland to report on the 1916 Easter Rising. She then travelled to France to lecture the troops in Dieppe, and in the following January, she went to the United States for the British Ministry of Information. At the end of the war, she returned to France and sat on the Imperial War Graves Commission. It was here she married the Australian officer (George Arthur) for whom she was working, and on their return to Australia she took up drawing seriously, and published another book of sketches called and about the "Circus".

Bertha was a member of the Royal Academy of Arts, and also of the Zoological Society at Regents Park. You can see her love of animals in her drawings. She used to take her niece, Tessa to the zoo and let her see behind the scenes, Bertha at one point getting Tessa to stroke a snake, just because Tessa was frightened of snakes. Bertha was living in Kew at the time. Bertha's husband was a Group Commander, much to brother Bertie's annoyance as he was only a Wing Commander. There is a family story that says that when Bertha was a young girl, Kitchener proposed marriage to her, but her father disapproved and put a stop to it as Kitchener was quite old at the time. It seemed that Burleighs great friend the one and only Lord Kitchener was in love with his daughter! Bertha did however have her ashes scattered on the north sea, perhaps in the hope she might re-kindle the relationship in the place where Kitchener was sunk and killed.

Unfortunately, three of Burleighs sons died during WW1. The first, Bennett died after wounds received whilst fighting with the Lancashire Fusiliers in Gallipoli in 1915 and his brother Robert died on 29th August 1916 in Thiepval. James was killed in action whilst fighting with the Argyll and Sutherland Highlanders on 12 October 1917, aged 21. The brothers are now remembered on a war memorial in Clapham. The youngest brother Bertie survived WW1 and became a Wing Commander in WW11, winning the military cross. Bennett who was 20 when he died is also remembered at the Lancashire Landing Cemetery, Turkey (Gallipoli) and at the Associated Newspapers Memorial in the crypt of St Brides, Fleet Street, London.

Robert, who before the war had followed his family into engineering, receiving scholarships and a diploma in the subject from the City and Guilds Technical College in West Kensington went on to join the Royal Flying Corp, the overland air arm of the British Military. Robert became a good friend of the Canadian airman and Victoria Cross winner, Wing Commander Barker, who gave an account of Roberts death in his correspondence. "… A pretty sad thing has just happened. An officer, Lieutenant Burleigh that I generally fly with was killed yesterday. Lieutenant Harry a new observer went up with him as I was busy breaking in a new pilot. I was in the air at the time and saw the fight. 4 Fokkers attacked him by surprise and killed him instantly. I immediately dived and shot one down but too late for I saw him crash to earth on our front line vertically with the engine on from 5000 feet. It made me sick to see it. My Hun planed back to his lines and also crashed.

The infantry pulled them into the trenches but they were dead. Their engine alone went 4 feet into the ground. I went up last night to the trenches and got all his valuables from his pockets and am sending them home. You know I had only agreed a few days back that if anything was to happen I would write his mother. This I am doing …"

In Wing Commander Barkers letter to Mrs Burleigh, he wrote "… Robert and I flew together until a few days ago when he was given a different observer. I have done many hours in the air with him. Day after day we carried on our work, and I never saw him anything but cheerful. One day not long ago he fought single handed six Huns when over on photography, and although his plane was badly hit, he landed perfectly. Robert was a true Britisher through and through. He accomplished feats in the air which Huns cannot understand possible; deeds which have given us command of the air. I have seen his grave, and when on leave I will give you one of my maps with the position marked…"

ROBERT BURLEIGH

True to his word, due to the fact that he couldn't get enough time off to go back to his own family in Canada, WC Barker spent Christmas at the home of the Burleigh family, 19 Glyn Mansions, Avonmoor Road, London. "…Mrs Burleigh … was bound that I would stay here and am only too glad to. I pay the ordinary lodging fee and in most cases have luncheon and dinner out down town. I like these people fine. They are a real good old English family .. .[Mrs Burleigh] has had awful bad luck. Lost her husband and two sons in this war so far. The youngest Lieutenant Burleigh has just arrived home from Salonica and Egypt and we have a great time together … as he knows the place well we get on fine. He is also going in for a pilots certificate…" , this son, James, who also won the military cross, was to die in Ypres that coming year. Robert is also remembered at the Knightsbridge Cemetery, Mesnil-Martinsart, Somme, France

James, the winner of the Military Cross, had his exploits described in the Edinburgh Gazette January 10th 1918; "For conspicuous gallantry and devotion to duty during a raid on the enemy's lines. He led his party with great determination, bombed a strong point which was holding him up, and caused considerable casualties, and when the signal to withdraw was given, carried back a badly wounded man himself and afterwards returned twice in search of others. It was entirely owing to his personal reconnaissance on the previous night that the enemy were located so that the raid could be planned." James is also remembered on the Tyne

Cot Memorial in Zonnebeke, Belgium.

Whichever way it worked out, it appears that Burleighs descendants of today are now living in all corners of the globe, from Scotland, England, Ireland and America to New Zealand, Canada, South Africa, Switzerland and Australia, with some of the descendants even adopting the double barrelled surname of Bennet-Burleigh. One of his grand children, Professor Michael Burleigh, became a journalist and historian, winning the Samuel Johnson Prize, for the excellent read, "The Third Reich, A New History".

Chapter 10 - Burleigh puts down his pen.

Unusually for a Fleet Street correspondent of the time, Burleigh neither reportedly drank nor smoked, and it was only in 1909 that Burleighs abnormally robust constitution fell to serious disease, when a case of double pneumonia brought him to his knees

STAFF DELEGATION FOR LORD BURNHAMS 80TH BIRTHDAY CELEBRATION (TELEGRAPH OWNER- CENTRE). BURLEIGH FRONT LEFT, TAKEN SIX MONTHS BEFORE HIS DEATH.

In his memoirs, a Colonel James, noticed, that during the Russian/ Japan conflict (1904-5) that the tempestuous Burleigh was "now visibly nearing the bottom of the wonderful stock of vigorous energy that for so many years had sustained him"; he again met him in 1911 in Tripoli, where he described Burleigh as a "...weary Titan, and it was pathetic to see how age and a recent illness had sapped an energy that in the past had seemed unfathomable."; it was his memories of Burleigh still trying to attain superiority in the field, that made James decide to quit the job whilst still in his prime despite the fact he saw the Great War looming.

Edward Lawson also known as Lord Burnham, the owner of the Daily Telegraph, reserved his major wars for professional reporters. Burleigh, during wars, travelled as "Milord" with magnificence and grace. Burnham claims "Burleigh to be the greatest of the Daily Telegraph war correspondents and possibly the greatest of all war correspondents. {though others would argue that his achievements were inferior to those of W. H. Russell or Archibald Forbes}. He was recruited through normal channels. Burleigh was then just over 40, squarely built, immensely strong, tough, enterprising, aggressive and, as I remember him and others found him, rather disagreeable". His life had been one of continual adventure. In all, he reported on 24 wars, mostly for the Daily Telegraph, seeing more action over 50 years than most living men, including professional soldiers. Generally in his life, Burleigh was not popular with his colleagues and was disliked and criticized by his rivals on other papers, 'largely because he was fiercely, and sometimes in their view, unscrupulously competitive'.

When Burleigh announced his retirement from the staff of the Telegraph, it came as little surprise to those who had witnessed his failing health, and less than seven months after his retirement dinner with the staff and owners of the Daily Telegraph (December 1913), Burleigh died at the Belle Hotel, Bexhill on Sea, Sussex, on 17 June 1914, just months before the start of the Great War which was to take the lives of several of his sons. His eldest daughter reported that he died of a broken heart, because he was too old to cover this war to end all wars. It was a rare type of man to receive the following tribute from Field Marshal Sir Evelyn Wood: " I much regret to learn of the death of Mr Bennet Burleigh, of whose accuracy, ability, courage, endurance, discretion, integrity, military judgment, and knowledge, patriotism, and tact, I have, from much personal observation extending over a quarter of a century, a very high opinion."

Another of Burleighs friends, a Dr Kusel, the one time head of customs in Egypt, noted a fitting tribute in a letter he wrote and published in the Daily Telegraph, "Sir, May I have the privilege of {testifying to} my respect for your late War Correspondent, Mr Bennet Burleigh. I was well acquainted with him, especially in the Sudan war of 1884-85. Well do I remember his cheery voice and his encouraging words to all of us on that memorable campaign, especially at that great conflict at Abu Klea, where we were so much outnumbered, and where one of our best and greatest soldiers fell, the late Colonel Burnaby of the Royal Horse Guards, whom I myself saw fall, exactly as your late Correspondent mentioned in his despatches".

Upon Burleighs death, King Edward set up a commemoration

committee, which Winston Churchill chaired in July 1914, during which a statue to his remembrance being erected in Glasgow was discussed. There was a pre-war project set up by Fleet Street to have a memorial tablet erected in the crypt of St Paul's in his honour similar to that of Melton Prior's and the other correspondents honoured there. The efforts towards the project were abandoned due to the war and when peace came, it was decided not to renew them. In another tribute, Falk, provides a fitting summary of Burleighs career, a reputation maintained by "vigorous writing, full blooded initiative and magnificent enterprise". At the turn of the century, these qualities began to be stifled by officialdom, and only in the latter stages of his career, did he experience being hedged around by every conceivable restriction. He adds, "had he lived six months longer, and remarked the way in which newspaper representatives, intended for the Front, were stupidly corralled, he might have argued that his honourable vocation was no more than a dying industry. As it was, merciful death closed his eyes seven weeks before the European tragedy began. I say "merciful death" advisedly for the war was to devour his three splendid sons". With the advent of the Great War, the era of the war correspondent was passing and the likes of Bennet Burleigh and his peers would not be seen again; this new style of total war, covering immense terrain with full censorship, meant a very different style of both soldering and reporting back. With the onset of war, Bennet Burleigh was soon forgotten, and in hindsight, it is hardly surprising as millions of young men died in a war that changed the face of the British Empire and the wider world forever.

The Obituary of Bennet Burleigh printed in The Times, June 1914, stated that "We regret to record the death of Mr. Bennet Burleigh, the famous war correspondent, which occurred at Bexhill yesterday. He had been in failing health for some time and for the past few days his condition was serious, but the end came suddenly. Mrs. Burleigh and two of his sons were present. With the death of Mr. Bennet Burleigh it may be said that the last of the old and picturesque type of war correspondents has passed away. Bennet Burleigh belonged to an age when the service of the great newspapers with armies in the field was left to certain hardy gentleman of fortune whose main journalistic asset was robust health, inexhaustible energy, and a picturesque imagination. In their way this class of war correspondent served their special public well, and a little mutual admiration among the limited membership of the corps placed them in the estimation of the less instructed public, in a category with the adventurers of the Spanish Main. The development of the art of war, with a rapid improvement in communications, brought into existence the censor as a check to the independence and the unbridled licence of the war correspondents. Burleigh worked both before and after the institution of military censorship in the true sense of the duty... Burleigh, when not employed on active service, largely represented his paper at Army manoeuvres and at military functions. He was not, however, what might be termed a constructive writer on any subject, nor had he any but superficial knowledge of military affairs... His "Highland Sergeant" and "Cockney Corporal" were always good journalism of a particular type".

The Daily Telegraph devoted an entire page to Burleighs obituary listing all his achievements and concluded that he exemplified the new era of war reporting - "corresponding by telegraph ... with unsurpassed skill, accuracy and judgement. In him there passes away one of the most intrepid and most brilliant journalists of his time. He had probably seen more warfare than any other living man over the last 50 years".

GRAVE OF BENNET BURLEIGH, BROOKWOOD CEMETERY.

Bennet Burleigh was buried in the non conformist, Chapel Hill Lawn section of London's necropolis, Brookwood Cemetery, Surrey, at 3pm, June 20th, 1914. His third wife Bertha, who passed away in

Belgium some 20 years later is buried in the same plot now marked by a 5'6" rustic grey Cornish granite cross.

In conclusion, it seems Burleigh was prone to assertiveness over military matters, but his judgment was seldom wrong, and his cheery optimism, ready smile, big voice and his tender nature endeared him to many. His favourite quotation from Milton suggests much, "What though the field be lost, all is not lost." His aims were to never be beaten with the news, to always keep his paper in the lead. He was a socialist, and a lover of argument, so much so that he " never was at peace except when he was at war."

I gave this book the title "Wild Bennet Burleigh" almost from the start; now it is ready to go to print, I have thought about it again; was Burleigh actually wild? He himself once described himself as a civilised nomad, a term I think that is perhaps a more apt reflection of the man and his career, my description of him being wild is in keeping with the feelings of his daughter, and is a term of endearment, a reflection of a life well lived.

SOURCES.

Adye, Sir J. (1925) Soldiers and others I have known. Herbert Jenkins.

Amery, L. (1953) My Political Life, Volume 1. Hutchinson.

Ashton, J. (1896) Hyde Park from Doomsday Book to date. Downey & Co.

Baker, G & Phillips, J. (Ed.)(1999) Essays in the History of Canadian Law. The Osgoode Society.

Baker, W.W. (1910) Memoirs of Service with John Yeats Beall. The Richmond Press.

Bartlett, A (1897) The Battlefields of Thessaly. Murray, John.

Baynes, Rev. A. (1900) My Diocese during the War. George Bell.

BBC4 (2007) Ian Hislops Scouting for Boys.

Bey, H (1903) Hector Macdonald: The story of his life. Stirling (Kessinger)

Bigelow, M.M (1959) The Confederate Attempt To Capture Johnson's Island. Bulletin of the Michigan Historical Society.

Black and White Budget (1900) Transvaal Special Vol. I-III. Black & White Pub. Co.

Blake, Col. J.Y.F. (1903) A West Pointer with the Boers. Angel Guardian Press.

Blue and Gray Magazine (March 1987) Johnson's Island Prison Vol. IV Issue 4.

Bull, R. (1900 est.) Black and White War albums Vol. 1-4. Black and White Pub. Co.

Bullard, F. Lauriston (1914) Famous war correspondents. Pitman and sons.

Burgess, J. (1911) John Burns: The Rise and Progress of a Right Honourable. Reformers Bookstall.

Burleigh, Bennet (1896) Two Campaigns: Madagascar and Ashantee. Fischer Unwin.

Burleigh, Bennet (1899) Sirdar and Khalifa or the Reconquest of the Sudan 1898. George Bell.

Burleigh, Bennet (December 1887) The unemployed. Contemporary Review.

Burleigh, Bennet (1900) The Natal Campaign. George Bell & Sons.

Burleigh, Bennet (1908) An address on old age pensions. National Liberal Club.

Burleigh, Bennet (1884) Desert Warfare. Chapman & Hall.

Burleigh, Bennet (1899) Khartoum Campaign 1898. Chapman & Hall.

Burleigh, Bennet (1905) Empire of the East or Japan and Russia at War 1904-5. George Bell.

Burleigh, Bennet (unknown) The Greek war as I saw it. Fortnightly Review.

Burleigh, Bennet (1897-1898) The Mahdi, or for the Victoria Cross. Walter Hill & Co.

Burleigh, Bertha (1937) Circus. Collins.

Burleigh, Bertha Bennet. (1935?) An Artist at the zoo. Collins.

Burnham, F.R. (1975) Scouting on Two Continents. Rhodesiana reprint Library.

Burnham, Lord (1955) Peterborough Court. Cassell.

Carnegie, M. & Shields, F. (1979) In search of Breaker Morant, Balladist and Bushveldt Carbineer. Graphic Books.

Catling, T. (1911) My Life's Pilgrimage. John Murray.

Cecil, H (2005) Imperial Marriage. Sutton.

Chesterton, G.K (1986) The collected works of G.K. Chesterton. Ignatius Press.

Churchill, R. (1966) Winston S. Churchill - Youth 1874-1900. Heinemann.

Churchill, Winston (2000) The River War. Prion.

Churchill, Winston (2000) My Early Life. Eland.

Churchill, Winston (2005) London to Ladysmith via Pretoria. Wildside Press.

Clarke, J. (2004) London's Necropolis. Sutton.

Collison, W. (1913) The Apostle of Free Labour. Hurst and Blackett.

Colvin & Gordon (1904) Diary of the 9th (Q.R.) Lancers. Cecil Roy.

Cooke, L (Sept 30th 1915) Article, *Newark Evening Star*, New Jersey.

Cutlack, F. (1962) Breaker Morant – A Horseman who made history. Ure Smith.

Davitt, M. (1904) The fall of feudalism in Ireland. Harper & Brothers publishers.

Denton, K (1980) The Breaker. Angus and Robertson.

Desmond, R. (1978) The Information Process. University of Iowa Press.

Doyle, Sir Arthur Conan. (2004) The Great Boer War. 1st World Library.

Doyle, A.C. (2007) Sir Arthur Conan Doyle, Memories and Adventures. Wordsworth

Duffy J. (2007) Victim of Honour. Rion Hall.

Duke, B & Knott, R (Ed) (1887) The Southern Bivouac Vol. II – June 1886 – May 1887. Avery & Sons.

Edwards, N. (1900) The Transvaal in War and Peace. H.Virtue & Co.

Estrange, Capt.W.D. (1999) Under Fourteen Flags. Somerled Publishing.

Falk, B. (1938) Five Years Dead. The Book Club.

Fraser, W.H. (2000) Scottish Popular Politics. Polygon.

Frohman, Charles, E. (1965) Rebels on Lake Erie. The Ohio Historical Society.

French, L and Byrd, R. (1929) The Big Aviation Book for Boys. McLoughlin Bros. (Kessinger).

Fuller, Sir T.E. (1910) Cecil Rhodes, A Monograph and a Reminiscence. Longman & Co.

Gardner, Major F. (1925 Est.) More Reminiscences of an old Bohemian. Hutchinson and Co.

Gooch, J. Ed. (2000) The Boer War. Cass.

Griffith, K (1974)Thank God we kept the Flag Flying. Hutchinson.

Haggard, R (2001) The Persistence of Victorian Liberalism. Greenwood Press.

Harvey, H (Sept 13th 1998) A Rebel Raid Foiled. Published in The Blade, Toledo, Ohio.

Headley, J. (1906) Confederate Operations in Canada and New York. Neale Publishing.

Horan, J. (1960) Confederate Agent, a discovery in history. Crown Publishers Inc.

Horwood, H & Butts, E (1988) Bandits and Privateers : Canada in the age of gunpowder. Goodread Biographies.

Houston, F (reprint 2010) Maxwell History and Genealogy. General Books.

Howse, Christopher. (2004) 150 Years of the Daily Telegraph 1855-2005. Ebury Press.

Hurst, G. (1942)   Closed Chapters. Manchester University Press.

Imperial Yeomanry Hospitals Committee. (1902) The Imperial Yeomanry Hospitals in South Africa, 1900-1902. Humphreys.

James, L (1929) Times of Stress. Murray.

Jerrold, W. (1916) Earl Kitchener of Khartoum: The Story of his Life. Johnson.

Johnson, P. (1978) Front Line Artists. Cassell.

Journal of the Royal African Society. April 1936 VOL. XXXV No. CXXXIX

Kent, W. (1950) John Burns: Labours lost leader. Williams and Norgate.

Kipling, R. (1990) Something of Myself . Cambridge University Press.

Kipling, R. (2003) The Light that failed. House of Stratus.

Knightly, Phillip (1975) The first casualty. Harcourt Brace Jovanovich.

Kusel, Baron D. (1915?) An Englishman's recollections of Egypt 1863-1887. John Lane.

Lane, M (1964) Edgar Wallace - Biography of a phenomenon. Heinemann.

Lecture Memoranda (1914) The dental art in ancient times. Burroughs Wellcome & Co.

Leviseur, Sophie. (1982) Memories. Human and Rousseau.

Long, R (1993) The Forty Dollar Pirate. Published in Seasons of Sandusky, Autumn/ Winter 1993.

Lucas, D.B. (1865) Memoir of John Yates Beall: His Life, Trial, Correspondence; Diary. Lovell.

MacDonald, A. (1887) Too Late for Gordon and Khartoum. John Murray.

The Magazine of History with Notes and Queries. Vol. 1 no 5 June and number 6 July 1905. Abbatt.

Menpes, Mortimer. (1903) War Impressions. A&C Black.

Military Commission. (1865) Trial of John Y. Beall, as a spy and a guerrillero. University of Michigan (Reprint).

Mills, E. (1999) Chesapeake Bay in the Civil War. Tidewater Publishers.

McCullagh, F. (1912) Italy's war for a desert. Herbert and Daniel.

Luo,H. (1976) The Correspondence of G. E. Morrison: 1895-1912. Cambridge Uni. Press.

Morrow, G (1908) Hustled History. Pitman.

Moseley, C. (1998) John Yates Beall: Confederate Commando. Bell Family Association.

Nevinson, H.(1923) Changes and Chances. Nisbet & Co.

NewYorkTimes.com. Various articles from archives.

Nesbitt, M (1993) Rebel Rivers: A Guide to Civil War Sites on the Potomac, Rappahannock, York, and James. Stackpole Books.

Neufeld, Charles (1899) A prisoner of the Khaleefa: Twelve years captivity at Omdurman. Chapman and Hall.

Nineteenth Century Fiction (Journal) Vol. 12 No.4 March 1958.

North America No 3 (1876) Correspondence respecting the Extradition of

Bennet G. Burley. Harrison and Sons.

Official records of the Union and Confederate Armies in the War of Rebellion.

Official records of the Union and Confederate Navies in the War of Rebellion.

Palmer, F. (1934) With my own eyes. Jarrolds Publishers.

Pearson, A. (1899) Pearson's Magazine. Pearson publishing company.

Preston, A. (Ed.) (1967) In relief of Gordon. Hutchinson.

Prior, Melton (1912) Campaigns of a war correspondent. Arnold.

Ralph, W. (1997) Barker VC. Grub Street.

Rappaport, E (2001) Shopping for Pleasure. Princeton.

Register of Officers of the Confederate States Navy 1861-1865 (1931) U.S Govn. Print Office.

Reynolds, E. (1947) Baden Powell. Oxford University Press.

Robinson, W.M. (1994) The Confederate Privateers. South Carolina.

Russell, D. (2005) Winston Churchill Soldier. Brasseys.

Severence, F, (Vol. IX 1906) The Johnson's Island Plot. Publications of the Buffalo Historic Society.

Sharf, J.T. (1978) History of the Confederate States Navy. The Fairfax Press.

Shaw, A (Ed.) (Vol. 26 July-December 1897) The American Monthly Review of Reviews. The Review of Reviews Company.

Sibbald, R (1997) The War Correspondents: The Boer War. Sutton Publishing.

Simonis, H. (1917) Street of Ink. Cassell.

Smith, E. (1924) Fields of Adventure. Small, Maynard & Co.

Smith, R.M. (1904) A Page of Local History. Pollock.

Smyth, J (2000) Labour in Glasgow 1896-1936. Tuckwell Press.

Southern Historical Society Papers of the War of Rebellion.

Spiers, E (2004) The Victorian soldier in Africa. Manchester University Press.

Spiers, E (Ed) (1998) Sudan, The Reconquest Reappraised. Cass.

Springfield, Lincoln (1924) Some Piquant people. Unwin.

Stetler, Professor – (1999) News Release. University of Guelph, Canada.

Stirling, J. (1903) Our regiments in South Africa. Blackwood.

Strand Magazine. Ed. Newnes, G. Vol. XXXII Jul-Dec. Is the British Climate Maligned?

Swift, H. (1929) A History of Postal Agitation. Percy Brothers Ltd.

The Nation (Journal) June 25th 1914. Obituary.

The Sketch (Newspaper). March 16th 1904 Article. Printed London.

Turner, Sir Alfred (1912) Sixty years of a soldiers life. Methuen & Co.

Turner, E.S (1956) Gallant Gentlemen. Michael Joseph.

Van Doren Stern, P. (1990) Secret Missions of the Civil War. Wings Books.

Villiers, F. (1920) Villiers, his five decades of adventure. 2 volumes. Harpers.

Warner, P. (1985) Kitchener. The man behind the legend. Atheneum.

Watson, Aaron, (?) A Newspaper Mans Memories. Hutchinson.

Watson, A. (1907) The Savage Club. Fisher Unwin.

Weinert, A. (1989) Defender of the Chesapeake: The story of Fort Monroe. White Mane Publishing.

Who was Who – 1897-1916.

Wideman, J. (1993) The sinking of the USS Cairo. UP Mississippi.

Wilkinson-Latham, Robert (1979) From our special correspondent. Hodder and Stoughton.

Wilkinson-Latham, Robert (2005) The Sudan Campaign 1881-1898. Osprey Publishing.

Williams QC, M (1891) Later Leaves. Macmillan & co.

Winstone, H (1982) Leachman: "OC Desert" Quartet.

Wise, S. (2008) The Blackest Streets. Bodley Head.

Witton, Lieut. George (Reprint) Scapegoats of the Empire. Angus and Robertson.

Wright State University, Ohio, Special Collections and Archives.

Wright, T. (1908) The Life of Col. Fred Burnaby. Everett.

Wright, T. (1936) Thomas Wright of Olney. Herbert Jenkins.

Thanks to:

Robert Wilkinson-Latham - author; George Newkey Burden - Daily Telegraph historian; Fort Delaware Historical Society; John Clarke, Historical Consultant, Brookwood Cemetery; Pete Massey for help with images, and my grandma Euphemia who inspired the 8 year writing of this book.

About the author.

Graeden Greaves is the triple great grandson of Bennet Burleigh. He was born in Manchester; attending St Bede's College before eventually graduating from Christ Church College, Canterbury. He then spent a few years working in London, before being summoned home to take over the family business. He is currently looking to move somewhere warm where he can spend his days surfing.

I am interested in any other photos or documents you may have for future editions of this book.
Contact the author: Graeden@live.co.uk

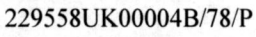